THE DISAPPEARANCE OF ETHICS

THE DISAPPEARANCE
OF ETHICS

The 2021 St. Andrews Gifford Lectures

OLIVER O'DONOVAN

WILLIAM B. EERDMANS PUBLISHING COMPANY
GRAND RAPIDS, MICHIGAN

Wm. B. Eerdmans Publishing Co.
4035 Park East Court SE, Grand Rapids, Michigan 49546
www.eerdmans.com

Book design by Lydia Hall

Printed in the United States of America

30 29 28 27 26 25 24   1 2 3 4 5 6 7

ISBN 978-0-8028-8349-0

Library of Congress Cataloging-in-Publication Data

A catalog record for this book is available from the Library of
Congress.

Contents

A Disappearing Discipline

John Henry Newman, speaking in 1852 on the idea of a university education, offers us our starting point: "If ethics were sent into banishment, its territory would soon disappear, under a treaty of partition, as it may be called, between law, political economy and physiology."* Newman's conception was a familiar one. Knowledge is a plural system, both comprehensive and specialized. The pursuit of "science" as a whole thus needs the pursuit of the full range of sciences. On that ground he argued in defense of the place of theology among the university faculties. His argument assumed, of course, that we have a priori knowledge of what the "full range" of sciences is. Reality must be presented to knowledge as already parceled out into so many recognized fields of inquiry. The evolution of academic life since Newman's day, with new disciplinary shoots emerging constantly from parent stems, complicates his question very considerably. Are the new disciplines discovered or invented? If they are discovered, the idea of a university seems to demand an ever-ramifying, ever-expanding structure of faculties, which is a desirable prospect for researchers, no doubt, but a nightmare to funders and administrators. If they are invented, how do we distinguish the essential core disciplines, the ones the university cannot do without, from those it can either take or leave? Newman saw the problem

* John Henry Newman, *On the Scope and Nature of University Education* (London: J. M. Dent & Sons, 1915), 57.

simply in terms of an insufficient plurality of sciences, omitting essential traditions of inquiry. Since no *reality* can be ignored, what happens when some *science* is ignored is that "the other sciences close up," to colonize the neglected field of reality. But the strategy of closing up is not an innocent compensation for the neglect. The colonizing sciences "intrude where they have no right"—that is, no intellectual competence. The rationality of the inquiry is therefore deformed, as the wrong questions are asked and the wrong analyses brought to bear.

In the Catholic University of Ireland, as in many universities since, this fate was in danger of befalling theology. Could it happen—Newman's first illustration—to Ethics?* If Ethics disappears, the subject matter, human conduct, cannot disappear. But it can be taken over by law, political economy, and "physiology" (mentioned as the parent faculty of psychology). That speculation seems prophetic. In our own lifetime distinguished universities have filled chairs of moral philosophy with economists. Two other illustrations Newman offers may strike us as more remote: "experimental science" could disappear into "antiquarian study," and "history" could disappear into "metaphysics." Those prospects are not on our horizon, but for his generation, when laboratories were a luxury and Hegel's shadow fell darkly over all the humanities, they could have seemed more probable than the displacement of Ethics.

By "Ethics" he did not mean "morality" or "moral reasoning." It is common enough to speak gloomily of the disappearance of moral behavior or of the diminution of moral reasoning. Philosophers discuss the "disappearance of moral knowledge" as an accepted feature of the current intellectual universe, and worry about a corresponding loss of the university's capacity to educate the young.** When I have told people the title of these

* "Ethics" will be spelled with an initial capital where it is used as the name of the discipline, and in other uses in lowercase.
** Dallas Willard, *The Disappearance of Moral Knowledge* (New York: Routledge, 2018).

lectures, they have often assumed that I was going to add to these expressions of anxiety about the vast moral losses of our age. It is a worthy and challenging theme; at other times I would gladly, and perhaps recklessly, have taken it up. My business here, however, like that of Newman, concerns the peril of *an intellectual discipline*, one to which I have devoted my working life. That peril may not appear quite so perilous as the other. Yet if the disappearance of Ethics as a reflective discipline does not make morality vanish from society, or moral argument from practical endeavor, it still has its alarming consequences. Morality unsupported by argument loses its authority; moral argument without sufficient base in reasoned reflection loses its conviction. Ethics defends the reflection that makes moral reasoning fruitful and moral practice credible. A society without Ethics is exposed by the poverty of its moral vocabulary and the rigidity of its moral arguments to the destructive forces of conflict and loss of tradition.

How, then, does the "disappearance" of Ethics occur? It requires no particular hostility from university administrators or rival disciplines. It occurs for reasons intrinsic to the study itself, when its practitioners lose sight of the realities they have to deal with. Ethics reflects on the living of human life, not, like anthropology or sociology, from a third-person observational point of view but from the point of view of agents who ask deliberative and evaluative questions about their practical undertakings. There is no describable *field of material data* that defines the study of Ethics, as, for example, the artifacts and inscriptions of ancient Egypt define the study of Egyptology. It is defined by an ambition to trace, clarify, and enrich the practices of moral evaluation and deliberation. In doing so it will often make use of descriptions supplied by more empirical sciences and subject them to forms of rationality tested by theology, philosophy, and law. It has its own range of descriptive categories, of course, some of which are unique to it: motives, decisions, sins, virtues, etc. But concrete practical reasoning needs other categories, too, if it is to get a purchase on the world. I cannot decide how properly to invest a sum of money simply by asking what my motive should be or what virtues it requires of me. I need an account of economic realities. That places Ethics in an exposed position in the academic ecology, lacking the power conferred on it by a closed field of data in which it is expert. Its expertise is not defined by its data, but by the distinctive lines of practical questioning that it applies to them. And it is these that are constantly at risk of deformation when it tends, as it does in both its traditional homes of theology and philosophy, to assimilate to other models of intellectual inquiry. At that point we see the proper discipline of Ethics disappear.

In these lectures I have two aims. The first is to notice three elements of Ethics that have in fact tended to disappear, and so to make Ethics disappear; the second is to explore the conditions of their reappearance. In the first three lectures I shall follow some well-beaten philosophical paths and recall a philosophical passage of arms that has now been rather forgotten; in the latter three the route is more theological, and taken more on my own responsibility.

An able younger scholar, seeking to help me overcome the confusions of old age, advised me recently to reread a book I wrote nearly forty years ago called *Resurrection and Moral Order,** promising that I would find "some quite good things in it." I followed the advice gratefully, and having overcome the predictable shock of encountering a younger self with younger manners, I decided that the positions defended there were strong enough to invite some further exploration. My principal claim in that book was that Christian Ethics must be a bearer of good news. I now presume to extend that claim and suggest that it is valid for all Ethics whatsoever. In doing so I hope to engage fruitfully with Lord Gifford's demand for a *natural* theology. Generations of lecturers on his foundation have found this demand sufficiently elusive, intriguing, or outrageous to require

---

* Oliver O'Donovan, *Resurrection and Moral Order: An Outline for Evangelical Ethics* (Grand Rapids: Eerdmans, 1986).

extensive discussion; to that I do not intend to add very much. But I should like to suggest that among the topics grouped under the heading "natural theology," the relationship of Ethics to theology must be somewhere very near the center. That, at any rate, was the view of A. E. Taylor, lecturing to this university on Lord Gifford's foundation just a century ago. I have kept *The Faith of a Moralist* open on my desk,* though his conception of the task differed from mine as greatly as our intellectual eras differ. In the late afterglow of idealism, he brought the resources of Ethics to supply a more secure foundation for theology, a legitimate project and well executed. I, on the other hand, bring the resources of theology to strengthen the foundations of Ethics, now manifestly itself in need of some good news.

In recording my thanks to the principal of St. Andrews for the honor of her invitation to deliver the Gifford Lectures, and to my colleagues in the Schools of Divinity and Philosophy for their gracious support, I must mention the conditions in which these lectures were delivered, wholly online, for reasons explained by the events that brought the world to a halt in 2020–2021. No lecturer could be imagined less suited than myself for this pioneering exercise (as it was then), and I was naturally disappointed to be confined to my study at home rather than enjoying the company of students and colleagues a few miles away in St. Andrews. By patient technological attention and careful guidance, however, the staff of the university facilitated what turned out to be an unforgettable experience, with participation from a worldwide public, much of it in remote time zones, which had grown hungry over the months of isolation for serious discussion of the most serious questions. To be the occasion for this reunion of thought was deeply moving.

Dunfermline
November 2022

---

* A. E. Taylor, *The Faith of a Moralist* (London: Macmillan, 1930).

ONE

The Missing Object

As a first step let us consider *the disappearing object* of moral thought. The famous opening words of Aristotle's *Nicomachean Ethics* declare that all action, practice, and aspiration "reach out for some good."* If we reach out for something, it must be there, or at least seem to be there. It is a reality, or we take it for one. But in Christian Ethics the good is very often not taken for a reality. So we have to ask how the real good has disappeared. Let us begin with an overview, uncomfortably cramped but otherwise familiar, of the legacy of ancient philosophy and theology on the topic.

THE REALITY OF THE GOOD

To know that something is real, or has being, we must be able to put a name to it, and to name something is to identify it, not simply as "this thing" or "that thing" but as a *something*, an instance of a kind of thing. Names of realities are not merely ostensive but classificatory. Adam could give his sons proper names, Cain and Abel, but as the first scientist he needed categories to give the *trees* their names: this creature was "a tree," as distinct from "a bush" or "a flower"; and it was "a sycamore," as distinct from "an oak" or "an alder," and (as he grew more expert) it was *acer pseudoplatanus* as distinct from *acer plata-*

---

* Aristotle, *Nicomachean Ethics* 1094a2.

noides. How, then, could Adam know what categories of things there really are? How could he know he could say, "This is a zebra" but not "This is a unicorn"? Because a kind of entity is known by its kind of goodness. Adam could recognize typical "perfections," the perfection of different rocks identified by differing component minerals and tensile properties, the perfection of living things by their activities and modes of growth. Trees could be distinguished by mature height, spread, leaf cover, depth of root, and longevity. If there had been no possible list of qualities associated with the growth and flourishing of trees, not only could he not have differentiated a sycamore from an alder but he would have had to doubt whether the name "tree" referred to any living kind at all. To speak of qualities is to speak of kinds of good appropriate to kinds of being.

"Every nature is good, insofar as it is a nature," was Augustine's way of expressing the unity of good and being.* A "nature," as Augustine spoke of it, was a concrete instance of being, specific or individual, spiritual or corporeal—that is, a particular that participated in some given universal. The nature of any thing, realized in measure, form, and order, was what made it beautiful, and beauty, for Augustine, was the category through which the idea of the good was first grasped. To be good was to be *good for* something, and beauty was the way beings were *good for* other beings, eliciting their responses if they were living beings, attracting their attention if they were animal life. Action could be accounted for entirely, he thought, as responsiveness to the good. This view was followed in general by the scholastic age. *Nihil appetimus nisi ratione boni*, it declared, recalling the opening of the *Nicomachean Ethics*. We strive for nothing except on the ground that it is good.

The unity of being and the good implies, inevitably, the nonbeing of evil. Augustine's conception, a reaction to the Manichaean dualist theology of "two first principles" of good and evil, held that there is only one "first principle," the supreme

* Augustine, *De natura boni* 1.

good, the principle whose name is being: "I am that I am." If to be good is to be something, and to be something is to be good, to be evil is *not-to-be* something. Evil is not-being something, not in the sense that it is simply nonexistent but in the sense that it fails to be something. *Not-being something* is different from *not being some* (specific) *thing.* In the second case, "is not" merely indicates the inapplicability of the predicate. A lecture "is not" a poem. One could imagine a crazy attempt to write a lecture in verse, but it would not make a good poem; one could imagine a lecture so rapturous and allusive that it had fine poetic qualities, but it would not make a good lecture. Any identity implies a large number of nonidentities, which is to say: if a predicate is truly applied to a subject, there are many predicates that cannot be truly applied to it. That form of negative predication is wholly innocent, merely an implication of the positive predication of something else. Evil is negative in a different way; it is the not-being of something that is expected to be, the nonfulfillment of pretensions. If someone says, "O'Donovan is no musician!" it may merely draw attention to the fact that my fondness for music has never gone beyond that of being an appreciative audience. But it might mean that when I open my mouth to sing, I produce an intolerable noise. To be *evil* is to be *no good at being* something one already "is" in some incipient or promised way; it is to be that thing imperfectly and insufficiently. Which introduces us to the important distinction between the *reality* of the good and its *realization* in event and practice. If Adam came on a sycamore stunted in growth, thin in leaf cover and with shallow roots, he might describe it as "a bad tree." By which he would not mean that it was something *other* than a tree, or a dead tree, no longer existing; nor would he mean that it belonged to a generic kind of tree that was, as such, evil, a monster tree. What he would mean is what is neatly expressed in our English idiom by saying it is "not much of a tree." It would be "bad" simply by failing to realize very much of the good of being the tree it really is.

This raises a puzzle over the delicate distinction which English, in common with many other languages, makes between "bad" and "evil." Broadly, the distinction seems to lie between what is not-good *accidentally* (but could quite possibly have been good) and what is not-good *essentially*, and could not have been good by any stretch of the imagination. The bad tree is bad *accidentally*—good insofar as it is a tree, bad insofar as it is "not much of" a tree. Are we to conclude from this that "evil" is an empty category, wholly without application, since everything there is, is good inasmuch as it is what it is? Yet in fact we talk about evil, and any philosophical antidualism that tried to stop us talking about it would be beating its head against a brick wall. But if "things" cannot be evil, what can be? The answer Augustine gave was, in the first place, *deeds* and *acts of will*, and in the second place, *states of affairs* originating from such deeds and acts of will. These could be "evil" *by their nature*—because there can also be a generic "nature" of events that happen and of acts that are done. There are acts of covetousness and spite; there are states of war and events of misunderstanding. Evil was a category *in history*, qualifying what happens and is done, not a category of ontology, qualifying what things are.*

If evil is attributable solely to things that occur and are done, not to things that are, good is attributable *both* to things that are *and* to things that occur. While a thing is good by being the kind of thing it is, an event, too, may be good. The being of a good thing is not necessarily eternal; good things may come to existence—on one of the six days of creation or on any day subsequently—and an action may be good in that it brings to existence, or to some fuller measure of existence, a good that already has real being. "Realization" of good is the distinctive

---

* One of the philosophically interesting aspects of J. R. R. Tolkien's famous fantasy *The Lord of the Rings*, currently under a critical cloud for the offense of being interested in good and evil, is that while it represents a world in which some kinds of thing are evil by nature (balrogs and orcs, for example), of which there are no examples in our world, it highlights the difference between these and the distinctively *historical* evil (Sauron and his designs) that is like the evil in our world in that it may be overcome by resistance, an evil performed by beings that might possibly have been good.

way in which acts and events are good. The idea of the good, therefore, has a temporal dimension, without being reducible to the idea of a succession in time. A new invention may be a good—but it is so not by virtue of the fact that it is *new*, but by virtue of the good that it *is*. If an aircraft is good, it is so because it is a good thing to be able to fly, and has *always* been regarded as such, though it was once assumed to be beyond the reach of human beings to realize. The act of inventing the aircraft was therefore a good act, by virtue of its realizing a practical good that had hitherto been out of reach.

This complex situation is complicated further by the recognition that acts may "realize" good in two distinct ways: by bringing about an instance of some good thing, or by *themselves* being an instance of some good act. For acts, though they are events of *doing*, belong to real kinds, and as such realize their own goods. An act of mercy is good because it brings about a state of affairs that is good for those who suffer from its absence; prisoners are set at liberty, sick people receive healing care, etc. Yet at the same time it is good simply as an instantiation of mercy, which of its own categorical nature is a good. Correspondingly, an act may fall short of the good in one of two ways. It may fail to realize the good intended, as when an ambulance hastens to answer a call but arrives to find the patient dead, or an argument meant to clarify things produces more confusion. Or it may fall short of the good by not *intending* the good that demands to be realized. It may be an act that overlooks the needs of the moment and pursues some wholly different good—like an ambulance that takes a long route to the accident so that the driver may see the fine view from the bridge in sunset. Or it may be an act the very intention of which is to frustrate the meeting of the need. We normally reserve the epithet "evil" for the last of these three possibilities, though there is a sensible question as to whether overlooking needs may sometimes not be an accident but an act, and of its nature evil.

Leaving the complexities of evil to one side, let us think first of the good as the *object* of practical reason—using "practical reason" in the most general way for our thinking about and to-ward acts, mental and physical, dispositions, attitudes, etc., and using "object" to refer to the *end* of action, the state of affairs to be realized. Practical reason is the approach of thought, both reflective and deliberative, to possible goods that may be realized. But if we have listened to the metaphysical tradition, we understand that "realizing" does not mean causing a good *to be* the good it is. The task of practical reason is not to conjure an unreality into being but to discover how a real good may be open to fuller realization. Practical reason in its deliberative mode often expresses itself in a language that makes no reference to the reality of the good, the language of obligation, signaled in English by the eloquently conditional verb "ought." This language views the object as simply *not there*, absent. It is serviceable for many immediate purposes: it identifies an object as a concrete historical state of affairs with no existence until action gives it existence; it focuses on the role played by action in bringing that state of affairs about. But the classical tradition warns us that such language, predicated on the opposition of presence and absence, of existence and nonexistence, cannot make ulti-mate moral sense on its own. Before any absence can become an object of action, it must be present to the imagination, and it cannot be imagined without having some kind of real and de-scribable form. We could not imagine something to be done without relating it in thought to some reality we know and can speak about. There are, of course, vaguely perceived absences that we cannot describe, but if we cannot describe them, we certainly cannot say that they "ought" to be present. "Ought" speaks of *what is owing,* and if we can speak with any clarity of a "debt" to reality, we can speak of the reality that defines the debt. The unreal cannot be owed to the real; it can have no debt of existence. Practical reason succeeds in its task when it grasps some real good, some possibility of fulfillment and realization implicit in the real world, that can be made explicit. From this point we understand better how "good" can be predicated of action itself. Experience is full of examples of acts and attitudes

directed to some good, which turn out to be bad acts and attitudes: when my loyalty to local tradition makes me suspicious
of everything foreign; when my urgent desire to protect threatened values excites me to violence; and so on. The good of an
action is a *complex* good, in which the transition from *admiring*
a real good to *conceiving* a good object for realization, and then
to *deliberating* on whether and how it may be performed, is an
articulated one, which may go wrong at more than one point.
A lack of moral sight, a lack of practical imagination, a lack of
comprehension of the circumstances and possibilities of action—all can drive the expression of the good out of its true
course. Our language of moral evil therefore needs a complex
discrimination that matches the multiple ways in which action
may fail. Moral inertness in a failure of love for the real good,
practical folly in assessing the possibilities, circumstantial blindness in understanding the context of action—each is a different
kind of failure. The judicial cast of mind, bent on condemning
and excusing, will always want to find an ultimate simplicity in
evil to match the ultimate simplicity of the good as being: when
mistakes and follies and lassitude are taken out of the picture, it
supposes, the *mens rea* can appear in all its purity. But that is why
the judicial cast of mind is an inadequate equipment for moral
reflection. If there is one point that justifies the difference between the natures of good and evil that the metaphysical tradition insisted on, it is that the supposed simplicity of evil forever
eludes our grasp. "Sin is multiple," as Aristotle declared.*

THE DISAPPEARANCE OF THE REAL GOOD

The doctrine of the reality of good occupied the mainstream of
the Western metaphysical tradition in the premodern era. There

---

* Aristotle, *Nicomachean Ethics* 1106b28. Augustine may be thought to
have reached the same point by the back door in confining the pure *mens
rea*, which has no cause but a "deficient cause" (i.e., no moral cause at all),
to the fallen angels (Augustine, *City of God* 12.8).

was, however, a minority stream of thought deriving from the negative theology of late Neoplatonism, which proceeded from the thought that God was beyond being and looked to find a form of godward engagement that transcended being. We encounter this negative tradition most clearly in the mystical writers of the Middle Ages, but it affects the scholastic tradition, too, through the voluntarism of the two twelfth-century Peters, Lombard and Abelard. By this route it contributed to shaping the major crisis of the Western intellectual tradition, marking the threshold between what we have come to think of as "antiquity" and "modernity." Out of it arose modern moral idealism, a widely diffused and popular philosophical tendency that is agreed by general consent to have found its most perfect expression in the thought of Immanuel Kant. For Kant, practical reason is founded on the "ought" alone, with no real good to support it. The negative implications of this assumption were expressed with startling clarity by Kant's follower, J. G. Fichte, who offered the following definition of Ethics: "Let the concept be the ground of the world. . . . The concept is a pure and absolute image *to which nothing corresponds*."* That is to say, Ethics requires a concept with no reality, an idea of *what is to be* that is wholly independent of *what is*.

In a crucial passage of the *Critique of Practical Reason*, Kant dissects the scholastic doctrine *nihil appetimus nisi ratione boni* by dividing the good into two quite separate ideas: on the one hand there is the "good" of *actual* objects, often used in the plural as "goods," which are perfections of natural being and the objects of natural appetite; on the other hand there is the *ideal* good of human action, which Kant prefers to call "the right," or "what ought to be."** An action could be good, or right, irrespective of whether it corresponded in any way to the real goods of the world or was capable of doing so. The only

---

* J. G. Fichte, *Lectures on the Theory of Ethics*, trans. Benjamin D. Crowe (Albany: SUNY Press, 2015), 3, 6.

** Immanuel Kant, *Critique of Practical Reason*, AK 5:59.

criterion is whether the action, if it *were* somehow realized, *would* contribute a new good to the sum of goods in the world, a question that no knowledge of actual goods, he held, could help us answer.* Natural goods that had actual being could not possibly be the measure of good in action. What is, *merely* is; what ought to be, *is not*. Kant had come to see actual being as a system of mechanical necessity, so that to conform to natural goods was simply to conform to the necessities of nature, not to exercise freedom. Freedom, the central pillar supporting Kant's dual structure of theoretical and practical reason, required a measure drawn solely from the principles of reason itself, presupposing no knowledge of what actual goods in the world there really are. What is actually, is necessarily, and so cannot determine freedom; what ought to be is what freedom set loose from necessity must choose to realize. We exercise free will only if our action is a kind of "making," for the faculty of will is a power to "produce objects." The measure of morality, then, is simply whether our "making" is coherent with itself. That is to say, morality is measured by the purely formal requirement that when we can imagine the object of our will as a universal law, we can still will it.

So the real good disappears, lost sight of in between the actual and the ideal. Actual good is constantly encountered in the world of nature through the material objects of our activity but can play no part in authentic practical reasoning. Earlier thinkers in the negative tradition had held that natural love of the good was morally suspect because of its inevitable suggestion of self-reference: if I recognize something as good, I recognize it as good *for me*; every thought of the good is thus compromised by self-interest. This was the anxiety of Fénelon, who wished to defend a supreme state of saintly ascesis in which we might even wish ourselves cut off from the good, that the good itself might be fulfilled uncompromised by our interest in it.** Kant was

---

* Immanuel Kant, *Critique of Practical Reason*, AK 5:15, 57f.
** The documents in the Bossuet-Fénelon controversy are too many

more canny. Self-reference is inevitable in a world of mechanistic action and reaction, and so our natural interest in natural goods is not in the least morally *suspect*. It is simply beside the point. It has no moral significance whatsoever. When we ask about the principles that should govern our conduct, we should simply ignore whatever goods we naturally admire and enjoy. Kant shares the mystical ambition to purify the focus of practical reason, but he plans to do it by philosophical clarification rather than by emotional ascesis, narrowing its conceptual scope to bar it from direct attention to actual goods, allowing it only an indirect critical reflection on our instinctive attractions and projects.

The familiar outline of Kant's theory that I have just sketched is likely to provoke objections from the expert band of the philosopher's specialist interpreters. In his introduction to the relevant volume of the Cambridge edition, Allen W. Wood protests "how inaccurate it is to take Kant's discussion . . . in the *Groundwork* as typical of . . . the kind of deliberation in which he thinks ordinary moral agents should normally engage."* Kant, more than any other thinker, perhaps, is liable to

---

to footnote and are mostly in French or Latin. The two-volume selection of Fénélon's *Oeuvres* in the attractive La Pleiade edition (Paris: Gallimard, 1983) contains the *Explication des Maximes des Saints* and the *Réponse à la Relation sur le Quiétisme*. Unfortunately, Bossuet's side of the controversy is not represented in the equivalent volume in that series, and readers must resort to the nineteenth-century *Oeuvres Complètes* (ed. Lachat and Guillaume). In the recent facsimile edition from Forgotten Books (2018), the *Divers Écrits sur le Livre intitulé Explication des Maximes des Saints* and the *Relation sur le Quiétisme* are found in volume 10. Secondary studies tend to start from an interest in the more glamorous Fénélon and typically underestimate Bossuet's achievements in the debate. Robert Spaemann's *Fénélon: Reflexion und Spontaneität* (Stuttgart: Klett-Cotta, 1990), though sharing this fault, compensates by bringing its author's fine philosophical mind to the questions. English readers who have encountered the debate through K. E. Kirk's chapter in *The Vision of God*, a hundred years old, will probably not need to be warned of its *parti pris*.

* Allen Wood, general introduction to *Practical Philosophy*, by Immanuel Kant, trans. Mary Gregor (Cambridge: Cambridge University Press, 1996), xxxiii.

be presented one-sidedly; and there is a good reason for this, which is that he virtually invites it. His great *Critiques* of theoretical and practical reason present their arguments in two steps, the "analytic," displaying the logic, and the "dialectic," bringing it into relation with its living context. The analytic is generally more dismissive of conventional common sense than the dialectic, so that interpreters may easily divide over which of the two has priority. For our purposes, we need not take a view, but may simply echo Kant's greatest moral-philosophical critic, Max Scheler: "Our purpose is not to criticise the historic Kant in his curly peruque."* The history of thought has a larger task, which is to point up the tectonic shifts of philosophical perspective that shape the intellectual landscape we presently occupy. The stark lines of Kant's structure can be filled out with some rather softer qualifications, as we shall see as we go on, but what matters first is the new paradigm, giving architecture to the mind-set of successor generations.

Endlessly quoted for its poetic force was the rhapsodic passage concluding the *Critique of Practical Reason*: "Two things fill the mind with ever new and increasing admiration and reverence . . . the starry heavens above me and the moral law within me. . . . I see them before me and connect them immediately with the consciousness of my existence."** It is curiously reminiscent of a sermon of John Chrysostom, who spoke of two teachers by which God is known, creation and conscience, the one striking the observer visually, the other reproducing its ef-

* Max Scheler, *Der Formalismus in der Ethik und die materiale Wertethik* 2–3; Eng. 6). I use my own translation of this work from the first separate edition published in Halle by Niemeyer (1913–1916), reprinted from the *Jahrbuch für Philosophie und phenomenologische Forschung*. A complete English translation by Manfred S. Frings and Roger L. Funk from the sixth edition appeared in 1973 from the Northwestern University Press, Evanston, IL; I add page references to that volume for the convenience of those with access to it.

** Kant, *Critique of Practical Reason*, AK 5:162. Kant, *Practical Philosophy*, 269.

fect internally, impressing us with our duties.* Both passages owe something to the Eighth Psalm ("What is man, that thou regardest him . . . ?"), beyond which I know of no direct connection. Yet between these rather similar ancient and modern reflections two differences leap to the eye. The theologian is led by the outer and inner objects of his attention to the knowledge of *God*, but the philosopher is led to the knowledge of *himself*. And where the theologian hears an "echo" of the cosmos in the conscience, the philosopher finds the two simply opposed: a world indifferent and inhospitable to freedom is confronted and defied by the practical freedom Kant describes as "personality." Suspended at a dizzying height above the world of mechanical necessity, the philosopher discovers himself to be at once an animal of infinitely small account in the universe, and at the same time a personal agent who transcends it with the infinity of freedom.

Such a picture cannot give us certain things we might reasonably look for in a model of Ethics. In the first place, it can never give us a human agent with a coherent span of life in time, for time is among the mechanical necessities of the world, and Kant's agency is perfected in a momentary instant of transcendent freedom, not over threescore years and ten. Youth and age, periods of life in which nature asserts a greater control, are threatening to freedom as Kant conceives it. In the second place, it cannot give us an informed and affectionate appreciation of the world's goods, the love of art and the love of friendship; there is no room for "good or bad enjoyment or pain," as Aristotle put it.** In the third place, it follows that it cannot allow the importance of admiring good people. "All my delight is upon the saints in the earth and on such as excel in virtue," boasted the psalmist (16:3 RV),*** but Kant cannot assent to

---

* John Chrysostom, *De Anna* 1.3, Patrologia Graeca 54:636.

** Aristotle, *Nicomachean Ethics* 1105a6.

*** Unless otherwise indicated, as here, all Scripture quotations come from the Revised Standard Version.

that. While he has a place for admiration, it is a provisional one, located among his thoughts on moral education, not among his thoughts on virtue. By being shown good models, he argues, we learn to recognize goodness; but that is simply a pedagogic exercise on the way to fuller moral understanding. Coming to know virtue for what it is, we reflect on its principles. Admiration may then fall as it will, for we are free of the influence of our models.

In these ways Kant wants us to disinterest ourselves systematically in "the goods." Can we actually do so? In certain circumstances and for certain purposes we can. Historians may detach themselves from their admiration and disapproval when reconstructing the narrative of past actors' deeds. Economists may disinterest themselves in what is desirable and what is undesirable when predicting alternative outcomes from alternative policies. Even philosophers may "bracket out" good and evil when they inquire into ontology or epistemology. One may disinterest oneself in anything at all, if one is pursuing other focused questions and seeking answers about other things. To exclude value judgments is just one among many uses of the technique of "reduction," as we have learned to call it, that accompanies all specialist investigation. But the law of reduction implies that once the special investigation is complete, and such answers as may be had are reached, we return to our natural disposition to know the world whole. Disinterest in good and evil may be a mode of inquiry; it is not a mode of existence. Existence is a good for all existing beings, and scientific investigators, too, have an interest in existence when they shut up their laboratories and go home for dinner. As existing human beings, they cherish the memory of past discoveries and seek the experience of new ones, knowing the value of discovery for conferring human significance upon their lives. But they do not formulate their memories and ambitions as truths of their science; they are content to inhabit the history in which they are immersed without attending to it scientifically. The popular myth of the brilliant scientist who is a disastrous human being is really a parable about the logic of scientific reduction. The astonishing feature of Kant's proposal was not that he thought disinterest in good and evil *possible*, but that he thought it *required of deliberating agents*. And even then it was not entirely possible, since the good was the inevitable object of appetite and desire. But it was both possible and necessary in moral reasoning.

Kant's quarrel with the reality of the good grew on ascetic soil, where moral thought was understood as a restraint on spontaneous action. Goods were thought to be of no moral interest because they were grasped spontaneously. They were therefore also thought of as undifferentiated, essentially the same, objects of impulse appealing to the pleasure principle. The older Western tradition had handled spontaneity in precisely the opposite way. It urged *reflective attention* to the goods spontaneously recognized, a disciplined quest to understand their underlying order and intelligibility. The task of practical reason was not to impose restraint on interest in the goods, a curb on their uniformly seductive appeal, but to reach a clear view of them, regarding both their permanent ontological order—spiritual goods before sensual, for example—and the ever-shifting possibilities for fulfillment offered by the opportunities of the moment, as when a moment of passing relaxation may be seized as the proper preparation for serious business in five minutes' time. To seize on the first good that offered itself would be a reflective failure, blind to the order of goods, blind to the opportunities for good at the present moment, and therefore neither wise nor prudent.

The Reassertion of Moral Realism

The standoff between ancient and Enlightenment approaches to ethics has often been described. Less attention has been paid to various more recent attempts to recover a view of the real object of moral thought. The twentieth century was persistently anxious about the perils of what it often called the "relativity" of ethics—a bad term, since all concrete moral judgments are bound to be "relative" to the situation that calls them forth and the agent that makes them; otherwise, they would not be moral judgments *by* anyone *on* anything. What lay at the root of the twentieth century's fear was the thought that ethics might turn out not to be *about* anything at all, but simply the arbitrary projection of the practical will of particular individuals or groups. This reduction of moral reflection, launched on German philosophy at the end of the nineteenth century by Nietzsche and on English-speaking philosophy forty years later by the logical positivists, elicited a series of realist reactions that aimed to overcome it without falling back into the hedonist materialism Kant had repudiated. I should like to recall one early and remarkably ambitious attempt, now little remembered, made in Berlin at the time of the First World War by the philosopher Max Scheler.

Bringing together three strands from the intellectual world of his time—the intentional psychology of Franz Brentano, the phenomenologist epistemology of Husserl, and the revival of interest in Augustine associated with Harnack and Holl— Scheler took issue with Kant precisely over whether there was a moral reality that could be known. Kant's restriction of practical reason to a formal critique of subjective impulse, he argued, had cut his thinking off from moral realities accessible to knowledge. Scheler's ethics was an "axiology," a doctrine of values, real values really "given" to experience. Revisiting his proposal at this distance, we have one major difficulty to overcome in understanding it: the terminology of "values" did not last well. The twentieth century was generally persuaded by Nietzsche that "values" are a creation of the will-to-power. As Jean-Yves Lacoste put it, "when we think in terms of values, devaluation is never far away."* Seriously reconstructive moral philosophers therefore disapproved of the term, because they thought it inevitably bound up with the voluntarism of economic exchange. But Scheler, who had read Nietzsche and appreciated much of him, resisted him on this point. "Values" were essentially real,

---

*Jean-Yves Lacoste, *Recherches sur la Parole* (Leuven: Peeters, 2015), 250.

though nonmaterial, objects of knowledge independent of our valuations, not creations of will. They were recognized by *Anschauung*—commonly translated "intuition," though "inspection" would often be a better choice. What intuition/inspection could do was to grasp empirical objects in space and time *as value bearing*. Some objects were essentially value bearing, some circumstantially, but in either case the value was both real and distinct from the object in which it inhered.*

In speaking of "values" rather than "the good," Scheler could stress the variety of forms in which the good presents itself—beauty in a work of art, nobility in a piece of conduct, strength in support, nourishment in food, charm in bearing, humility before the recognition of truth, etc.—while keeping his distance on the plural expression "the goods," which was captive to ma-

---

* Though Scheler will not usually say that values "are" (*sind*), or that they have "reality," he will speak of the "being" (*Sein*) of values as "essential" (*wesenhaft*) objects, or as "ideal objects" as distinct from "actual" (*reale*). He classifies them as *Wesenheiten*, essential realities, involved in *Wesenzusammenhänge*, essential implications. A value is not to be confused with a "thing" (*Ding*); yet it is, before all else, an object of *Erkenntnis*, knowledge, and *Erfahrung*, experience. This knowledge-experience is not of "inner" or "introspective" objects of knowledge; it is an "outer" knowledge of the world as distinct from ourselves, a world in which values are "objective" (*objektiv*, but not *gegenständlich*). When we "know" the values that a person or thing "bears," we know a *Tatsache*—that is, a "state of affairs" or even a "fact." In his clearest statement of the ontology of values, he declares: "To be sure, the pure or absolute facts (*Tatsachen*) of intuition are quite different from facts that must run the gauntlet of a series of observations (in principle infinite) before they can be known.... The difference is not between 'experience' and 'non-experience,' or as is said, 'the presuppositions of experience,' which inevitably must lie outside experience, but between two *kinds* of experience, a pure and immediate experience and an experience mediated by the organising function of the subject who has the experiences." Scheler, *Formalismus*, 47; Eng. 52. Scheler's reluctance to ascribe "being" to values while ascribing factual reality to them is easily understood if "being" is taken to mean "actual concrete being," and the expression "ought-to-be" is taken to mean "ought-to-be-realized." *Sein* in Scheler is often synonymous with "existence." His criticism of Spinozan ethics turns on his rejection of the thesis that *Sein* (i.e., mere existence) is a good in itself.

terialist and consumerist overtones. And it allowed him to escape one feature of Augustine's doctrine of the good that made
him nervous, that of the unitary being of the supreme good.
Scheler was even prepared to admit some quasi-Manichaean
claims: we have direct cognition of "negative values" as well as
"positive" ones, and we should not equate good and evil with
absolute and relative being.*

Two features of Scheler's doctrine should be emphasized.
In the first place, intuitive knowledge of value is not open to
explanation in terms of any *nonmoral* knowledge. Values are
not complexes of nonmoral properties. Like other objectivists
of the period, Scheler appealed to the analogy of color, which
is taken to be a property of objects irreducible to any other kind
of property. This was the thrust of his attack on what he saw as
one of Kant's most troubling legacies, the materialist empiricism of the nascent science of psychology, a field in which he
was remarkably well read. In the second place, the difference
between knowledge of empirical properties and knowledge of
values puts an end to Kant's distinction between theoretical and
practical reason. Theoretical reason, for Kant, is about *knowing*; practical reason, about *doing*. But for Scheler moral reason,
too, is a kind of knowing. And this has one dramatic implication: there are *realities* in the world that are known to reason
only as it is actually engaged in a well-directed exercise of will.
This thought, which can be traced back to Saint John's Gospel
(7:17), has been very seminal in subsequent twentieth-century
philosophy. An existentialism such as Heidegger's may possibly be read as reconstructing knowledge within the framework
of active existence, while another form of the idea appears in
the so-called "second-person point of view" or "agent perspective," which enjoyed some popularity in later twentieth-century
moral philosophy.

It was a heady moment in the history of Ethics, which left a
bigger imprint on Western moral thought than the official histo-

* Scheler, *Formalismus*, 166–67; Eng. 166–67.

ries allow, when the empty formalisms of Kantian rigor and utilitarian prudence were flooded with the light shed from a galaxy of hitherto unimagined objective values.* One culturally important implication was that cognitive and aesthetic values were restored to respectable objectivity, and indeed to a place near the pinnacle of the hierarchy of values. Developed optimistically into a theory of ever-expanding recognition of values, moral objectivism could regard science and art as the vanguard of moral progress. "As life develops, individually or more universally, with increasingly differentiated functions of hearing, seeing, tasting etc., it is encountered by new and more complex qualities emerging from the universe, and more differentiated feeling is matched by new and more complex values."** But the triumph of intuitionist objectivism was short-lived. Fundamental speculative questions, always present in the Western tradition of the good though suppressed by Kant's ascetic discipline, rose up to confront it.

1. The first question concerned the way we conceive the complex "order" in which values are supposed to present themselves. There are lower values and higher; there are values that strike us immediately and others that appear only on reflection; there are values particular to ourselves and our history, and others that we recognize as universal; there are values that we can only appreciate and admire, and other values that we can act upon. Order is the key to understanding the values and the entities that bear values. To take some familiar examples, we do not understand what money is, let alone what good it is, if we do not understand that it is for exchange; we do not understand what friendship is, let alone what good it is, if we do not understand that it is not "for" anything else at all. Order is also the key to answering deliberative questions about how values may be

* Scheler was not, of course, alone, though his impact eclipsed the other German disciples of Brentano. English-language philosophy had learned of "intuitionism" from Sidgwick, Moore, and Prichard.

** Scheler *Formalismus*, 158; Eng. 157. Scheler's occasional flashes of cultural optimism appear to have no foundation in an account of historical progress or even of personal development.

realized or implemented in action. Scheler understands deliberation as a process of *selection* among values, picking out the important, the relevant, and the presently possible. This process is supposed to end up with a resolution on just one value that can be the predominant ground of action for *this* agent at *this* moment. What kind of a judgment is contained in the decision to terminate deliberation and to act? Is it a judgment that there is only one thing to be done, and nothing else left to think about? That would mean we could never terminate deliberation short of certainty, or in the case of shared deliberation, unanimity. Is it, alternatively, a judgment about how the objective values bear upon us *in this situation*? But what sources of understanding are available to tell us just what "this situation" is? We are left, at any rate, with an idea of decision that is quite ill-defined. And this follows from an "order" of values conceived in terms of simple prioritization of higher over lower, relevant over irrelevant, rather than as the description of the moral field, grasping the relations that frame the moment in which we have to act.

2. From this there follows a second question. We attribute goods, as we have said, both to real things and to events, and among events both to states of affairs and to acts. There are goods we *admire*, as subsisting apart from us and available only to contemplation; there are goods we *enjoy*, by participating in them through an actual historical relation; and there are goods we *enact* in the exercise of our agency—achievements, good company, and mercy, for an example of each. How are these different types of goods connected in deliberation? The first type may not appear to enter deliberation at all. We discern the beauty of a work of art by intuition; it is "given" to us, and that is that; no specific deliberation and action follow from it. It is possible to maintain that the good *to be done* is deliberatively prior to the good *to be enjoyed*. This is the order of priorities maintained by Kant.* It is also possible to maintain the oppo-

---

* The more recent moral philosophy of the Aristotelian revival, which also lays claim to be "moral realism," has moved sharply back in the Kantian

site. "If I take a hat off the stand and put it on my head," Scheler observes brusquely on one occasion, "the point is to have my hat on."* Elsewhere, we find him saying that the value of the state of affairs is itself subordinate to the value of the *person*.** It is clear that Scheler intends these rules of priority to be universal. But how do they relate to the rules he most commonly employs for ordering values: sensual values subordinated to vital, vital to mental, mental to spiritual? And how do either of these sets of rules comport with his general prejudice in favor of particular values over universal?

3. A third question then follows. An objection sharply expressed by Jean-Yves Lacoste claims that Scheler "wants to know too much about values and to know it too quickly," and "has overlooked the worldly conditions of affectivity that prevent the perpetual parousia of values."*** If goods are in action, are they not also in temporal sequence? And if so, how can we think of them appearing only in disjointed and absorbing *moments* of moral experience, now this value, now that? Can we acquire learning about values as we grow older or as the human race progresses? There is a strong intuition, which it would be difficult to shift, that moral experiences are accumulative and that there is a moral wisdom that comes through reflecting on experience. One experience leads to another, and viewed together they constitute a total experience of the good in life that is more than the sum of its moments. What was decided earlier will often shed light on what has to be decided later. It is not,

---

direction on this point: *only* activity supplies the ultimate end that justifies all states of affairs. Even inquiry into truth, as is argued by Talbot Brewer, aims not at knowledge but at the activity of attending to reality. See Talbot Brewer, *The Retrieval of Ethics* (Oxford: Oxford University Press, 2009).

* Scheler, *Formalismus*, 126; Eng. 126.
** Scheler, *Formalismus*, 384; Eng. 370.
*** Jean-Yves Lacoste, "Du phénomène de la valeur au discours de la norme," in *Le monde et l'absence d'œuvre et autres études* (Paris: Presses Universitaires de France, 2000), 123.

of course, that there are no immediate answers to immediate moral questions; it is simply that the answers are not dissociated and separate but build up into something greater through mutual implications and cross-references. The old saying of Solon of Athens that we must call no man happy until he is dead, is a sharp way of highlighting the moral significance of the total life experience. Once we have engaged with the complexity of "values" in the plural, are we not bound to push the horizon of our moral questions back to *the* good, *the* way to follow, *the* guide to life? But that will take us where Scheler was not prepared to go, into an account of the relation of the good and history.

To put that relation briefly: the idea of a *final* good implies a notion of history as a unifying moral structure, not simply a succession of moments. And the unity of history depends on that feature of Plato's and Augustine's doctrine that made Scheler anxious, the unitary reality of the good. That is why religious moral teaching has usually started from that point. When Jesus of Nazareth was approached by a young member of the ruling class who addressed him politely as "good master" and asked him what he was to do with his life, he replied with the words "One there is who is good" (Matt. 19:17). Clearly, he did not mean that nothing and no one in the world can be good in any sense. But the cheerful promiscuity with which we apply that epithet to a master, a logical argument, an act of courage, or a glass of wine has to be stopped in its tracks. We are directed back to the *presuppositions* of the pluriform good. When in 1940 Dietrich Bonhoeffer (who read Scheler) wrote the first preparatory essay for his never-written *Ethics*, its thesis was: "Only one reality!"* To this theme we shall have to return. But as an earnest of intent, we close this lecture by observing how the unity of the good is implied in religious practice through worship.

* Dietrich Bonhoeffer, "Christ, Reality and the Good," in *Ethics*, Dietrich Bonhoeffer Works 6 (Minneapolis: Fortress, 2005), 40.

WORSHIP AND THE GOOD

That a considerable literature has grown up around the relation of worship to ethics in the past generation is something for
which we may be grateful. It has tended to emphasize the function of worship as a *formative* social practice: "liturgy" is a social
exercise that shapes the moral thinking of those who engage
in it.* Undoubtedly, this is one aspect of the truth. The term
"worship" does indeed speak of liturgies, individual and social,
which are importantly formative for their participants. But it is
also an expressive practice, witnessing to experiences of moral
disclosure that have already taken place. "Who will show us any
good?" asks one of the loveliest of the Hebrew Psalms of moral
reflection (4:6 RV). And whether it is asked skeptically or ear-
nestly, that is a real moral question, rooted in moral experience,
probing the conditions on which the good is susceptible of disclosure. That antecedent disclosure is what worship responds
to in the first instance. The question in the psalm is followed
directly, as Hans Ulrich likes to point out, not by an answer but
by a prayer: "Lift up the light of thy countenance upon us!"**
Conveniently cognate in English with "worth," worship is best
understood as the disciplined exercise of a convergent and
unifying view of the good. A variety of experiences of goods,
natural and historical, is connected in worship to a single origin and goal, a supreme good that is neither to be enjoyed nor
performed but simply admired, a sovereign agent with whom
we engage in dialogue, addressing and being addressed. The act
of worship traces the goods of nature and history back to their
origin in this primary agency and then reenvisages the good of
human existence itself as a good of agency.

---

* For an eminent example, see Bernd Wannenwetsch, *Political Worship:
Ethics for Christian Citizens*, trans. Margaret Kohl (Oxford: Oxford University Press, 2004).

** Hans Ulrich, *Wie Geschöpfe leben: Konturen evangelischer Ethik* (Mün-
ster: LIT Verlag, 2005), 86.

If the only agents we knew were ourselves, the attribution of good to an agent would always be secondary. For we are, as Augustine remarked, a great question to ourselves. We should be forced to look for goods initially in the world outside ourselves, in its vast storehouse of things and states of affairs, and work backward from these to the acts that realize them, and finally behind the acts to the agents who perform them, so extending the use of the term "good" through its three successive applications. The good agent appears at the end of the road, as it were, caught in the headlights of good acts, but remains for the most part in the dark, hidden and elusive. To learn to appreciate the good of a human agent consistently, we need to acquire a wide and intimate experience of that person, and even when we have acquired it, we can still be surprised or disappointed. But in the act of worship, the whole direction of the inquiry is reversed. We first encounter the agent whose activity sheds light on all experiences. In that light we relearn experiences that were familiar already but imperfectly understood. It is often supposed that the greatest obstacle to worship is our consciousness of bad experiences, whether our own or those of others. But in fact, it is just as difficult to see behind the surface of good experiences. Nothing is more common than the loss of a sense of moral context in a moment of triumph and celebration. Joy and suffering are both opaque, presenting impermeable surfaces and denying us a view of what lies behind them.* We are forced to probe them for their coherence. There is a multitude of narratives, plausible and implausible, available to those who seek to understand why they experience the good and evil that they do: their bodies are sending them messages, their subconsciouses are giving them instructions, their destinies are summoning them, their enemies are bewitching them, their past mistakes are catching up with them, and so on. What these narratives have in common is the invocation of a kind of

---

*On this see especially Jean-Yves Lacoste, *The Appearing of God*, trans. Oliver O'Donovan (Oxford: Oxford University Press, 2018), 152–75.

agency, for agency is the nearest model to hand for any meaning we may seek "behind" experience. Many of these shadowy
agencies are imaginative self-projections, created either to re-
inforce personal agency directly or to excuse and extricate it
from its weakness. The discipline of ordered worship imposes a
control on these projections. It offers in their place an encounter with a real agent, whose purposes are not merely disguised
versions of our own purposes. "God's will" affords not only a
meaning of the experiences we have had and are having, but
a purposed future good sufficient to evoke our own agency.

The endlessly generative texts of the Hebrew Psalter point the
way. Three moments in worship are repeatedly depicted there.
First, they recount dramatic experiences of good and evil:

> When evildoers assail me,
>   uttering slanders against me,
> my adversaries and foes,
>   they shall stumble and fall.

The emotional tension of the Psalms owes much to the sheer
variety of the experiences they recount, especially evil ones,
which are made to stand in close conjunction with the source
of good. Second, they celebrate the consistently communicative
good of divine agency: "The LORD is my light and my salvation. . . . / The LORD is the stronghold of my life." And third,
they find in this a ground of practical confidence:

> The LORD is my light and my salvation;
>   whom then shall I fear?
> The LORD is the stronghold of my life;
>   of whom then shall I be afraid?

Those three moments, quoted from two contiguous lines of
one poem (Ps. 27:1–2), recur throughout the literature. And in
the transition from the second to the third we see the character
of the Psalms as distinctly *moral* texts. They reimagine life as a

practical possibility, an undertaking, in fact, of robust cheerfulness and promise.

Only very occasionally do the Psalms explore specific patterns of moral behavior:

> Who does not put out his money at interest,
>   and does not take a bribe against the innocent.
>   (Ps. 15:5)

More usually they are concerned with the *framing* of the moral life, exploring its possibility and satisfaction, leaving the practical patterns to be understood. As they do so, they look forward in time. Infamously, Hebrew lacks an unambiguous future tense; yet the forms of prediction are everywhere recognizable, sometimes clothed in the English present tense:

> And now he lifts up mine head . . .
> and I offer in his dwelling
>   an oblation of gladness
> I sing and utter praises.
>   (Ps. 27:6, author's translation)

They look forward also in petition, "Arise, O LORD; O God, lift up thy hand" (Ps. 10:12), and in exhortation,

> Wait for the LORD;
>   be strong, and let your heart take courage.
>   (Ps. 27:14)

One might even say that the sequence of the tenses—the past of experience, the presence of God's justice and kindness, and the future of a responsive and fulfilled existence—forms the essential structure of psalmody in the Hebrew tradition. But—and here is the decisive point—their view of the future is not simply a predictive one; it grasps the future in moral freedom as an open space for human agency. For the Psalms the original application of "good" is to an *agent,* and to the *unitary* agent, the divine. To speak of the good in any of its many other forms is to presume upon the unity of meaning and purpose already operative, to discern that human agency and its world are held in place by the divine agent, always in action and always at rest.

TWO

The Missing Frontier

A meeting heavy with symbolism, happily recorded by an eyewitness, occurred in Weimar in October 1827, when the eminent Hegel dropped in for tea with the yet more eminent Goethe, now elderly, and conversation turned to the topic of "dialectic." The philosopher explained the term to mean "the regulated, methodically cultivated spirit of contradiction which is innate in all men, and which shows itself great as a talent in the distinction between the true and the false." This produced a rather tart response from the old man: "Let us only hope that these intellectual arts and dexterities are not frequently misused and employed to make the false true and the true false!" Hegel parried by saying that such use of dialectic would be "mentally diseased," only to be dismissed with the reply, "I therefore congratulate myself on the study of nature, which preserves me from such a disease. There we have to deal with the infinitely and eternally true."* What offended Goethe was not the commonplace thought that knowledge may often be reached by a zigzag course through contradictory assertions. It was the idea that knowledge was, in the end, no more than the sum of the contradictions involved in reaching it. Knowledge must be decisively achievable in principle. One who knows something about nature *is at the far end* of an inquiry, beyond the ebb and flow of argument, occupying the observer's view-

---

* J. P. Eckermann, *Conversations with Goethe*, ed. J. K. Moorhead, trans. John Oxenford (London: Dent, 1930), 243–44.

point. Dialectic admits no observers, only participants, and defers an absolute truth until the end of history. By "dialectic," in effect, Hegel meant history as *productive of truth*. That confrontation of an eighteenth-century philosophy of nature with a nineteenth-century philosophy of history was pregnant with much twentieth-century thought, from Lenin to Einstein.

From Nature to History

In the first lecture we attempted to recover the link asserted in ancient philosophy between good and being: something is good by virtue of what it is, not by virtue of what it is not. This brought us face to face with two related challenges. One was to conceive a harmony in the different ways we experience good, through admiration, through enjoyment, and through action. The other was to bring into view the temporal conditions that must govern our experience of the good if we are ever to enact it. Now we take up the second of those challenges, approaching the frontier of time, another dimension of moral thought that tends to disappear.

It can seem that the good and time are detachable. The goodness of God is self-sufficient and eternal; our encounter with it must be receptive and contemplative, essentially unaffected by the temporal conditions in which we find ourselves. "Thou hast no need of *my* goods," as the earliest Latin translations thought that the psalmist said (Ps. 16:2): "thou" as the *eternal* good, "my goods" as belonging to *this* moment, *this* agent. The good is complete in itself, approached through pure contemplation, and to worship and enjoy it is to be lifted above the changing time of life and action. Yet such pure enjoyment, divorced from the time of life and action, is not something we can easily conceive of. In actual experience, wonder comes to us, reality dawns on us. Discovery is an event, and it confronts us not only with the question, "What is this?" but with the question, "What is to be done about it?" Knowledge of the good commands our "existence," but existence is oriented to engagement in the world.

Worship of the good may even be viewed as a *first action*, a point at which contemplation, focused on the good that has no need of our good, passes into active response. That is the logic that leads from the real good to our engagement with time. Something is good *for us* not only by virtue of *what it is,* but by virtue of *when we meet it,* by its coming first, or its coming next, or later. We speak of a "right moment" for a given action or experience. The same thing done or experienced earlier or later would not be as good. This "first," or "next," or "later" cannot be separated from the real good we experience. For reality has a temporal, not only an ontological, dimension. The conclusion from this, if we hold firm to the connection of good and being, sounds paradoxical: reality itself must be temporal; there must be such a thing as *new* reality. What kind of reality could that be?

Time may be thought of simply as a lens through which eternal regularities are observed. Watch a rosebush for a year, and you will learn about its annual cycle of leafing, budding, flowering, and dying back. Watch many rosebushes for many years, and you will learn of their other natural characteristics: their mature height, their life span, their varieties of habit, their tolerance of frost, and conditions for successful growth. All this information will be essentially unchanging; whenever and wherever it is learned, it will be the same; the phenomena I see in my rose bed are more or less those that my grandfather observed in his. The rose-growers' handbook can safely go through many reprintings. Time makes no difference to natural processes; it merely displays them. In learning these natural processes, we learn of natural finalities. We learn that the rose is a form of life developing in a certain direction to a certain end, in search of nutrition, growth, and reproduction, following a natural course from immaturity to maturity, and then to senescence and death. Yet these finalities, too, are perfectly regular; the display comes back in the end to where it began. As Goethe wrote:

Laß den Anfang mit dem Ende
Sich in eins zusammenzieh'n.*

* Johann Wolfgang von Goethe, "Dauer im Wechsel," in *Sämtliche Werke,*

One way of putting this is to say that the rose has a life but not a "history." Time reveals the rose; the rose does not reveal time. We sometimes hear talk of a "circular idea of time," but in fact it is not time that is circular but nature. Time simply displays nature's circularity. We might better refer to a "refractive" idea of time as a prism through which the light of nature is broken up into its spectrum of sequential moments. Nothing about time's refraction of nature could have caused Goethe the slightest unease. As a novelist and dramatist, he was used to displaying nature through time.

But what if we turn from the rosebush to another plant? We are advised by Jesus of Nazareth to "learn the parable of the fig tree" (Mark 13:28, author's translation). From that, he suggests, we may learn about times *that are coming*, for when the fig goes into leaf, we shall know (in the Eastern Mediterranean at least) that summer is near. Late in leafing because it fruits first, the fig is a promise of summer when other trees, earlier in leaf and later in fruit, are inactive. Here the demonstrative relation of nature and time is reversed. A natural form of being responding naturally to its context becomes the lens through which we mark the progress of time on a wider front, and can anticipate the whole complex of seasonal events.

And to speak of this wider, more embracing finality, we need to speak not of "maturity" but of "fulfillment." A maturation is observable and recognizable, a fulfillment is not. A "fulfillment" may be described as the end of an end, a higher teleological finality superimposed on a lower one. We humans have an organic finality of health and strength, which matures somewhere between our twentieth and our thirtieth year, but beyond that threshold it is not all downhill; our effective activity, which depends on acquired experience as well as strength, is at its height, perhaps, at around fifty. And beyond these two horizons of achievement there is a finality in existence, the attainment of

---

Band 1, Sämtliche Gedichte (Zürich: Artemis, 1950), 512f., "let the beginning and the end draw together into one!"

which cannot be predicted and measured as the other two can. Fulfillment is never recurrent, always anticipated. We know that we may either succeed or fail in life, but we never know whether we have succeeded or failed. "Call no man happy," said Solon of Athens, "until he is dead," for success in life is not measured by the intermediate finalities alone. Yet even then, we must reflect, it can only be a crude conjecture, for a fulfilled existence has to have some relation to personal aspirations and we do not know another's aspirations from inside. Stretching our view beyond the single human life, we may think of the goals of a human culture, or even of world history as a whole. Then it is even clearer that "fulfillment" is something we can only view from a position of relative unfulfillment. It is a frontier we have to approach, not a territory we can have possessed. The idea of fulfillment is formed by our being immersed in time, situated at the moment we are, unable to narrate more than a fragment of the past, while looking forward to a future that is at once a closed book and the focus of all our practical striving. All this is implied in Jesus's parable of the fig tree: as the sprouting of the fig leaf anticipates the coming of summer, so certain indicative events may help us anticipate the fulfillment of history. But anticipation is something we have to learn how to do. Fulfillment is something we have to learn how to see. We do not do it by projecting patterns from our narrative of the past into the future. It is not like predicting regularities.

In the historicist thinkers of the nineteenth century, "evolution" was a name not only for the observable or conjectured process of modification in specific organisms but also for an overarching narrative of biohistory. "Narrative" is an ordering of events with a logic of its own, not a form of *classificatory* description, but a *sequential* description that is necessary to the knowledge of historical agency. "History," correspondingly, is what we know by narrative. Yet the thought of a narrative of *all* history is irresistibly mysterious, precisely because our immersion in time forbids us narrative access to the future and "fulfillment." A comprehensive world-historical narrative

from beginning to end, such as Augustine attempted with some
methodological self-awareness, and his medieval imitators with
rather less, is not what critical historians have in view when they
reflect on their craft. They deal in segregated and partitioned
episodes; they tell us only one of many possible histories at a
time. They can inquire objectively into the history of commer-
cial expansion in eighteenth-century Britain, or into the development of political structures in ancient Greece, but not into
history as a whole and not into future history, for that includes
what is still to become of us. "History" in the singular, as they
understand it, is simply the art or method of objective inquiry
to establish the narrative of any particular history. When philosophy conceives the idea of a single all-embracing world history,
a totality implied by all the partial histories historians study,
we have to wonder how such a history could be told, by whom
and to whom. Only, it would seem, a revelation that accompanied the unfolding of history itself could give an indication of
its overall direction.

   The idea of a comprehensive world history was not a new
invention of nineteenth-century philosophy. Before the birth of
modern philosophy in the mid-seventeenth century, all studies
were thought reducible to history. What was new in the nineteenth century was the idea that history could be interrogated
philosophically, and that philosophy could correspondingly assume the form of history. For Hegel, the "philosophy of history"
was wholly implicated in the "history of philosophy." But as
philosophy was drawn closer to history, it made contact with religious and moral concepts of ancient pedigree. The question of
the success or failure of a human life as a whole was entertained,
as we have seen, by Solon in the sixth century BC; the idea of a
final resolution of world history was entertained by the author
of the book of Daniel in the second century BC. "For Jews demand signs and Greeks seek wisdom," said Paul (1 Cor. 1:22),
meaning by "signs" events disclosing the end of history. Jesus of
Nazareth made the claim that "the time is fulfilled" (Mark 1:15).
So a large number of moral and theological questions that were

closed to philosophy by the Renaissance division of intellectual responsibilities were opened up once again to philosophical colonization. The nineteenth century produced philosophical treatments of original sin, revelation, salvation, and eschatology. While Goethe was celebrated as a freethinker, Hegel passed in his day for an orthodox Lutheran.

And in subjecting history to their interpretation, the philosophers consciously attempted to erase the boundary separating the study of history from the study of nature. Though there are some valid historical generalizations that may be methodologically useful for testing historical reports for credibility, history records deeds, attitudes, and beliefs that were what they were when they were. Historians display the quiddity of each fragment of the human experience of time. This fragmentariness in the historical object is precisely what the Hegelian philosophy of history sought to overcome. Bringing the whole of worldly history into a consistent pattern of meaning, it pressed history back into the mold of nature, treating it as susceptible to regular observations and predictions, and so interpreting its fulfillment as a kind of natural maturity. History became naturalized.* And from that development the social sciences were born, those always questionable, never eliminable increments to the study of nature that grew out of nineteenth-century historicism.

The adventurous colonial expansion of philosophy raised the question of who would gain and who would lose more. Theology, bewildered and often indignant at having its sacred *temenos* invaded and occupied, benefited incalculably. The twentieth century saw an intellectual reanimation of theology that could never have occurred without the challenge. For philosophy the legacy was more ambiguous. While gaining huge patronage over a progeny that included psychology and the social sciences, and a much greater political influence, through

---

* For this outcome of the Hegelian project, see especially Jean-Yves Lacoste, *Experience and the Absolute: Disputed Questions on the Humanity of Man*, trans. Mark Raftery-Skehan (New York: Fordham University Press, 2004), 120–26.

Marx, than it had known since Plato left Syracuse, it was forced
to learn the truth of one historical generalization that has some
validity: consolidating an empire is always more difficult than
annexing it. By the beginning of the twentieth century, philosophers were looking to retrench their frontiers and strengthen
their ontological and epistemological foundations. What sur-
vived of "history" within these narrower bounds were the discovery of a psychologically experienced "subjective time" and
the idea of a "historicity," so-called, in which temporal succession is deprived of significance and we are left with the formal
character of an *event* as distinct from a *thing*, an ontology of
pure happening, a kind of "becoming here."

ANTICIPATION

What of the losses and gains for Ethics? The philosophy of
nature and the philosophy of history had both offered Ethics
support, claiming to supply it with essential concepts drawn
from the regularities of organisms or the unfolding progress of
history. Shall we dare to say that Ethics had been pampered?
That its appearances of rational order were in fact all borrowed
clothing? Certainly, the withdrawal of those supports left Ethics
in need of new weatherproofing against the winds and rains
of skepticism. It was possible to think that the whole involve-
ment of Ethics with future-facing projection was a sophistry.
C. S. Lewis dismissed it satirically: "Goodness = what comes
next!"* Many sophistries did, indeed, spring from the idea; the
good cannot be reduced to possibility, any more than it can
be reduced to determinate fact. Yet when the sophistries have
been unmasked, we cannot disentangle moral thought from the
thought of future time, and that is because a practical disposition is inseparable from a future-directed intention. Reflective
thought moves backward and forward at will, but existence
moves only out of the past into the future. The contribution of

---

* C. S. Lewis, "Evolutionary Hymn," in *Poems* (London: G. Bles, 1964), 55.

Heidegger to Ethics (a contribution he had little desire to make) was to recover the past and future as "horizons" of the present, an insight always implied in Augustine's theory of time but lost sight of in the unbounded present tense of idealism, which even Scheler did little to correct.* Action follows the same direction. It is not, as is sometimes thoughtlessly suggested, a matter for "the here and now." The agent reflects on how things have been in order to deliberate on how things shall be. To live in an unbounded present without the definition of a past and a future would be like one of those dreams in which something has just happened and something has urgently to be done, but one cannot work out what.

About this temporal positioning of moral thought, three clarifications should be made.

First, to deliberate,** which is to think about *what to do*, is to adopt a certain mental stance in relation to future time that is different from other possible stances. Not only is it different from recollection of the past and feeling of the present, it is also different from other kinds of anticipation. It looks forward to an immediate future upon which action is to be ventured. We act "in the present" only to the extent that the present has an opening to the nearest future. What is presently a deliberation in the mind is shortly to become a performance in the world, and the nature of deliberative thought is to imagine it as it will

---

* According to his theory, the mental acts of memory and anticipation are an exact mirror image of each other (Max Scheler, *Der Formalismus in der Ethik und die materiale Wertethik*, 340–57; Eng. 328–44). Yet he can suggest a history of the discovery of values (515; Eng. 493–94), can refer to "an eternal progress from power and constraint" as "the being and acting of persons . . . [which] is the goal of community and history"—a "noteworthy train of thought" in which he finds a mandate for technologization (525–26; Eng. 505)—and can even imagine "a kind of world-historical distribution of the whole moral labour of the race, the final outcome of which will be unique, something greater than mortal eyes have hitherto seen" (565; Eng. 543). But this thesis is expressed only in passing suggestions; it is never developed.

** On this topic, see my *Finding and Seeking*, Ethics as Theology 2 (Grand Rapids: Eerdmans, 2014), chap. 8.

be when performed. This is not "anticipation" in the normal sense, which has to do with predicting events that are presumed to be going to happen anyway; when we deliberate a course of action, we presume to *decide* on the event. There is a term of art, "protention" (better spelled with a *t* than an *s*), that perfectly captures the deliberative imagination of the future: a "protention" is an incipient "intention" to act. Intelligent protention is bound up with sensible anticipation, of course, but it adds to it the active engagement of our agency.

Second, though we are not always consciously deliberating on what to do, it is an existential necessity, even in the course of our more reflective thought, that we have a deliberative horizon marginally in view. It is always there, always liable to present itself in a moment of threat or restlessness. And while a focused deliberation is exhausted in the formation and execution of the act it is directed to, this existential deliberative horizon is not confined to a focused content; it is never exhausted. It is a deliberative concern for *life as a whole*, for what we are to become. And so it extends beyond protention to limited anticipations of longer-term future conditions over which we have no power to decide. One who devotes himself or herself to the practice of some art—let us say, music—must envisage a future (which may never be realized) where certain conditions for the practice of that art are met: a future in which he or she has gained greater skill, in which the sacrifices the art demands are made, in which the ever-present risk of losing the necessary skills and competences is borne. Will there be such a future? The devotee cannot know. But it must be imagined as possible.

Third, to protect it from the subversion of skepticism, moral life needs confidence in an *ultimate future*. So, at least, thought Kant, rather in tension with his primary account of moral reason as conformity to the form of law. Since law offers a critique of instinctive appetites, the conscientious application of law requires, he thought, a higher object of appetite, the expectation of a perfectly reconciled moral state in which the critique has completed its work, a state of "blessedness." To pursue any good as we ought to pursue it, we need to pursue it in the context of a Last Good, a goal to which other goals point forward. And here we need a power greater than anticipation. We need a moral faith, a belief that the ultimate course of events will in the end prove hospitable to, and vindicate, the efforts of moral life and action.

So moral reason needs not only imaginative aspirations but a cognitive relation to the future, but that is not at all like a cognitive relation to the past. The past is determinate and known, can be recollected and narrated. The future, though not beyond anticipation and faith, remains essentially unknown. Never by any inflection of the mind can we think of the future as we do of the past—not, that is, without wholly sacrificing historicity, projecting ourselves into some imaginary lookout post that has views in both directions, so that the future appears as a kind of alternative imagination of time, a "History of Middle Earth," as it were, which we can dream of but not enact. Freedom has to encounter the future as open and receptive, ready to be determined by how we shall act upon it. Yet it is equally an implication of freedom that we can act *fittingly* toward the future horizon. We are not doomed to shoot all our arrows in the dark; we may anticipate enough to aim our deliberations responsibly. How can we do that? By prudent construction of anticipations from experience of the past, for anticipations are projections of acquired experience and depend for their validity on the continuity of experienced events. The virtue of prudence, which means, of course, "foresight," is a capacity to select from past experience what may be valid for the exploratory probing of the future.

Anticipation is only an approximation to knowledge. The hard knowledge on which it calls is always knowledge of the past, the experience of processes repeated with such regularity that we may safely project them into the future. Some of these processes are so generally immune from interruption that we can agree, without feeling we are stretching a point, that we "know" something will happen in the way that it always has. It would be too scrupulous to hesitate over a claim to know the hour of sunset tonight or of high tide tomorrow. But most predictions allow less security than that; and some people can predict them more reliably than others. It is an aspect of prudence to be judicious in prediction, knowing what factors are relevant, how heavily each should weigh, and how strongly the regularities govern the contingencies. It is an aspect of prudence to know how judicious other people's predictions are. Sometimes we claim knowledge of the future on other grounds than anticipation, from revelation or from second sight. In that case our conviction rests not on the object's predictability but on a subjective capacity or an authoritative communication. But all forms of future knowledge, of all degrees of certainty and uncertainty, are subject to one condition: it is not a knowledge of *fact*, as knowledge of the past is. "Fact" means "done." To know what "will become" is by definition different from knowing what has been done. Which is why we should not imagine time as a line that stretches out on either side of us; rather, it is an interface between what is already closed and what is still open. The teasing questions of science fiction about whether, if we knew the future, we could change it, are susceptible of a short dismissal: if we knew the future *as fact*, we would not know it *as future*. There are no "facts" about the future; knowing the future, which is by definition open to action by ourselves, others, and God, is not the same as knowing facts. And "change" is not a category that is in place either in respect to the past, which is closed, or in respect to the future, which is open. The possibility of change relates only to the world that accompanies us out of the past into the future, the world, in other words, that we *presently* receive and act upon.

A system of Ethics that rests everything on prudence, like the "utilitarianism" that dominated the imagination of the English-speaking world for two centuries, is not an effective way of attending to the future good. It replaces the good accessible to action on the near horizon, which is the real concern of prudence, with a remote future good supposed to result from an indefinite series of causes and effects that the next act will initiate. But long-term outcomes are much less open to view than immediate ends, so instead of anticipating what can be anticipated, it advises us to anticipate what cannot be anticipated. And what could possibly count as a "final" end in such a series? How long is the "long run" by which we are advised to measure the short run? Prudence within its competence is indispensable to rational agency, but its competence reaches no further than the predictability of events. An ethical system that makes everything hang on prudence comes down in the end to betting everything on the regularities of nature, which are our only basis for longer-term anticipations. J. S. Mill drew the consequence unblushingly, when he concluded that to *observe* a utilitarian ethic was simply to obey the most universally agreed rules of action, the distilled results of an experience that was most likely to predict the effects of action appropriately. The supposed conflict between ethical systems promoting future consequences and those promoting conformity to formal rules—"teleology" and "deontology" in the jargon of the textbooks—turns out, then, to be more of a collusion. One might even say that utilitarianism was the *original* "formal ethics," conceived as Kant conceived his version, as a way of talking about how to act when one suspends the knowledge of real goods open to action in real time.

How, then, ought Ethics to take note of the future? It could decide to embrace an ethic of prudence with all its limitations, knowing that it confines moral reason to the predictable short term, where anticipation has some purchase. The routine calculations that the predictability of nature allows us, we may say, must be the limit of our ambitions for moral responsibility. While it may be wise (in a speculative way) to remember that all societies, all planets, and even galaxies undergo crises that render the ordinary exercise of practical reason impossible, we cannot adapt practical reason to such contingencies. We may even think it imprudent to admit such reflections into public discourse. Those who correctly warned of the economic collapse of 2008 were publicly branded "irresponsible." If uncertainties that could deter us from planning next week's diary are sufficiently remote to be ignored, had they not better be ignored? Schleiermacher thought that Ethics was a description of life in "peaceful conditions."* When conditions are not peaceful, we must simply renounce the competence of moral reason. What plausibility this recommendation can claim derives from the obviously limited scope of public deliberation for the common good. But moral reason is not confined to the public sphere, and it cannot afford to sever its connection with our interest in existence. The existential horizon stretches not just for a week but for a life, at least, and why not even for eternity? Sometimes we want to benefit generations to come; sometimes we want to enter the kingdom of heaven. Prudence can certainly not get us that far. And if there is no other resource than prudence for addressing these horizons, we are doomed to despair.

But what of the opposite policy, to act without reference to consequences and to clothe ourselves in a purely normative ethics of duty "though the sky may fall"? We shall still not have done with the future. Kant, the great theorist of the moral law, saw the need for moral faith, a belief that conscientious application of moral reason would be vindicated in the long run by history—if not by a happy outcome, at least by the reconciliation of the sensuous with the moral nature. In the last analysis, goods of action and goods of experience must be reconciled. To act under the guidance of a norm that is not weakened by the paucity of our future knowledge, we must at least know this one thing about the future: that by so acting we shall, as Jesus of Nazareth expressed it, "save our souls." But such a faith needs a ground in experience. Let us name that ground, whatever it may be and wherever we may think to find it, as a "promise."

* Friedrich Schleiermacher, *Introduction to Christian Ethics,* trans. John C. Shelley (Nashville: Abingdon, 1989), 38.

We return in a moment to the forms that such a "promise" may take in experience. But we must first pause over the suggestion that these supposed alternatives for moral thought—one relating action to duty, the other to the prospect of future outcomes—are not alternatives, but converge. We are all too familiar with the textbook theory that these two modes of thinking correspond to rival *theories* of practical thought, "deontological" and "teleological," each professing to give a total account of moral reason on its own formal theoretical base. These theories turn out to be typical academic abstractions such as no living and acting human being could ever hold. Yet there is a phenomenon of moral thought that the two-theory theory has noticed, a divergence in *style* of moral deliberation. Let us speak (without prejudice) of a *mode of responsibility* and a *mode of opportunity* in deliberation. One may be led into a train of practical thought by a set of actual circumstances and relations that requires consideration before one can discern a course of action. There are roles and needs and commitments to be taken stock of. One may, alternatively, be led by a goal that summons us to realize it. There are questions like: "How should a head teacher in a multiracial school respond when charges of racial bias are brought against a staff member of minority ethnic background?" But there are also questions like, "Where may we find a long-term solution to the problem of funding the humanities in universities?" It appears that some people are disposed by temperament or training to frame their questions more in the one form than the other. But it also appears that different contexts of action tend to present their questions more in the one form than in the other.

Either mode of deliberation allows for a broader or a narrower range of factors to be taken into account, and we tend to admire those agents who, thinking in either mode, are capable of integrating broader with narrower views. Someone may indeed need to act "as a head teacher," but that person will be more admired if at the same time he or she can act "as a fellow teacher" and "as a human being." One may indeed have to look to the funding of the humanities, but one will be admired if one can be seen, at the same time, to take a wider view of what the university can and should contribute to society as a whole. And while we admire competence and thoughtfulness in either of these two modes of deliberation, we would not acknowledge competence in anyone who was incapable of accommodating considerations raised in the other mode. So a conception of what is required of a role must be flexible enough to appreciate the need to respond to opportunities, while a vivid sense of the opportunities in a situation must be able to take note of existing responsibilities. Competence in deliberation, from whichever end we approach it, requires attention to all material factors, and many material factors look both ways and can be seen as either forward-looking or backward-looking. To the opportunist, every responsibility suggests an initiative; to the responsible, every initiative recalls a responsibility. To be incapable of appreciating responsibilities, or to be incapable of appreciating opportunities, would incur a judgment of deliberative incompetence, or in plainer language, pigheadedness. A third observation: while admiring competence in either mode of reasoning, we admire especially those who are versatile enough to adopt either mode as appropriate. The head teacher is expected to have a clear sense of the responsibilities of that role, but especially admirable is the head teacher who, when he or she retires, is capable of scanning the horizon for interesting possibilities of doing other valuable things. Which suggests that deliberation, well conducted, moves constantly *between* the past and the future horizons, correlating the two in different ways for different occasions. And what goes for individual agents goes for cultures too. In the course of a generation, our own has swung, or so it appears to one who has lived through the change, from reckless opportunism to regimented censoriousness. Both are deeply deficient postures. They are deficient because they are in some measure irrational, as any attempt to stop practical reason in its movement between past and future horizons is bound to be irrational.

PROMISE AND DESIRE

All moral experience takes place in a temporal framework. In deliberation we engage with the interface of future and past, attending to the goods that approach us as opportunities and to the goods that lie behind us as a framework of moral responsibility. Goods generate freedom and also elicit discrimination. For most deliberative purposes neither past nor future need be known extensively. A certain experience of life, a certain sense of open space ahead, is often enough. To underpin them, and to vindicate the unity of the good in action and experience, the disciplines of worship encourage a reflective recollection of goods lying further in the past and the hope of an ultimate future. Deliberation needs sustaining especially on the side of the future. The horizon of the future is heavy with threat, not only buoyant with hope, and despair can easily erode it. We are challenged by the moral teaching of Jesus to grasp the future in two different ways, both by seizing its immediate opportunities and by fixing our minds on the ultimate horizon of God's kingdom. At the same time, we are told to "take no thought for the future"—that is, the future that is neither immediate nor ultimate, beyond calculation but not beyond impractical speculation. There is nothing contradictory in this; it corresponds precisely to the logic of deliberation and to its difficulty.

The disappearance of the future good, like the disappearance of the real good, deprives Ethics of its object. It may disappear into mere predictive anticipations based on past experience; it may disappear into the vacancy of a wholly unknown future that can neither be welcomed nor loved. Goodness does not equal "what comes next." And yet goodness *must* "come next," and not merely be looked back to, nostalgically. But for that to be the case we need a promise.

About such a promise it may seem that there is nothing general to be said. We may be tempted to shrug our shoulders and conclude that if promise is given to experience, it must be given by revelation, recognized by faith, unamenable to any description that might help us recognize it. But what cannot be described at all, cannot be thought of. If, in the light of past promises claimed and believed, there is at least the outline of a phenomenology of promise that sheds light on our ordinary deliberations and actions, faith and understanding may, after all, be mutually reinforcing, here as elsewhere. So let us think for a moment about one experience, as universally human as could be wished, which has played a large part in theologians' attempts to describe the human response to revelation. That phenomenon is *desire*. Henri de Lubac famously captured its significance in his phrase "the natural desire for the supernatural."

Though Neoplatonic metaphysics often tries to lift desire out of time and present it as a purely ontological yearning for being, we ought to dismiss, as simple misdescription, any purported desire that makes no reference to the future. The closest parallels to desire are anxiety and hope, which are also future related. But while desire engages with the future, it does not *know* the future. It entertains *possible* futures, knowing that they are merely possible. Sometimes what we desire as possible may also seem practicable, in which case the connection of desire and deliberation is immediate: we ask ourselves whether we should act to satisfy our desire, or not. But desires are often impractical, opening up no path for deliberation to follow. We can desire, for example, the presence of someone who has died. Yet what is impractical is not unthinkable; we can desire miracles, and we can know clearly enough what it would be like to receive the miracles we desire. In that form desire may still *assist* deliberation. It can lead us to believe, to hope, and to pray, even where it cannot lead us to act in other ways. Desire must always have some object that can be judged (in the widest sense) possible. If it has not, it ceases to be desire and becomes despair. "Delight becomes death-longing when all longing else is vain," as Yeats wrote.* The point we reached in the last lecture is therefore reinforced by the phenomenon of desire: the good that can

* W. B. Yeats, "From 'Oedipus at Colonus,'" in *The Collected Poems of W. B. Yeats* (London: Macmillan, 1933), 255.

absorb us and elicit our powers of agency is something *real*, in the broadest sense—that is, it belongs within the universe, and it offers, at least ideationally, something *realizable*.

Yet desire has to do with a good that is absent. To desire implies wanting, in the literal sense of being without. It is tempting to lose sight of this, and so to lose sight of the limits of desire within practical reason. Desire does not include every kind of evaluative appreciation. If it did, its object would be the good as such, not the absent good. The price paid for this expansion of desire into a master concept of appetition and admiration is to lose sight of its experience *as an affection*, a feeling of a distinct kind, different from "liking," "enjoying," "willing," and so on. Desire is a specialized emotion. Not all doing expresses desire. We can do deliberately what we feel no desire to do, and while desire may be a precipitating factor that carries us from reflection to deliberation, it is only one such precipitating factor. A sense of duty is another. Other strong emotions may take its place, as when we strike out in anger, weep in sorrow, shout in jubilation, etc., all without the assistance of desire and sometimes in the teeth of a desire to control ourselves.

An "absent" good is not a good that simply *has no being*. A good can be wholly present to our knowledge, but unfulfilled, pregnant with possibilities. That is how good excites desire, and so excites purposes of action. It promises more of itself. Sometimes that "more" is an immediate possibility, waiting to be realized, sometimes a distant object of longing. But in either case there is a difference between satisfied desire and a pleasant surprise. The desired good is ideationally present to us, desirable because it is implied within a good known in experience, promising a fuller implementation of it. For desires to be intelligible, they must be grounded in constellations of known goods. Elizabeth Anscombe famously asked philosophers to weigh their reaction to someone who claimed to desire a saucer of mud, hardly part of any good we are familiar with at all.* To understand a desire we must understand the place of the object in the universe of

* G. E. M. Anscombe, *Intention* (Oxford: Blackwell, 1957), 70.

goods. We desire to marry because we are in love; present love makes desire for future marriage intelligible. The more desire is focused *on what is not there*, the more arbitrary and pointless it appears. A musician may sensibly desire to complete the *Unfinished Symphony*, of which Schubert left two perfect movements out of the classical symphonic four. It makes no sense at all to desire to complete Sibelius's Eighth Symphony, of which not a note that is definitely attributable survives. Without a real and known good, the desire to supply what it lacks is contentless. But one cannot desire to supply what it lacks unless one's enjoyment has been cut short. It is possible to feel that Schubert's *Unfinished* is simply perfect as it stands, and the romantic aesthetic no longer requires a symphony to have four movements; in which case one cannot desire to finish it. The *gap* in the good must be *there*, just as the good itself must be there.

So the speculative question posed by desire is this: How do the goods we love come to have gaps in them? The answer brings us back to the refractive effect of time in displaying goods. Goods reveal themselves in temporal sequences, first appearing and then disappearing, and sometimes reappearing. Desire is the heightened awareness of the *coming and going* of goods, a distinct emotional response to temporality. But seen like that, the gaps in the good are not only promises waiting to be fulfilled but reminders of things that were good and have passed away. Desire has its two characteristic notes, one of hope and one of loss. Desire born of loss allows for sad gratitude; desire born of hope allows the prospect of satisfaction. Nothing in desire itself can tell us that the note of hope is more fundamental than the note of loss. Nothing in desire itself can assure us that a loss is open to recovery, and that all desires can be satisfied in a final reconciliation of goods. If the loss we feel when someone dies is to be recovered, we shall need to be told about it. It cannot be extrapolated from intimations of promise in general historical existence. But if we *are* told about it in a way that invites belief, then we shall find that the promise of an integrated final satisfaction addresses the desires we ordinarily feel, and gives them a weight of importance they could not otherwise have.

"Ordinary historical existence" is not "history." It is only an intimation born of natural recurrence. "History" is world-time conceived as convergent, purposive, and ultimately reconciled with itself. Whatever promises we may see in ordinary recurrences and hopes, the promise of history has to be given in a historical event, a pointer within history to the end of history. And since history never repeats itself, our belief that we know something of history and its end will, until the end of history, remain belief—not without grounds, but without decisive verification. We shall know that a reading of history is true when its predictions have proved true once and for all—which is at no point *in* history. The clue to history, then, if we are to find one, must be given in a supremely meaning-bearing event, or a constellation of such events, which convey promise and elicit faith.

That thought had its roots in the world of Alexandrian Judaism, open on the one hand to the teleology of Plato and Aristotle, open on the other to the historical thinking of the Jewish Scriptures. In the Letter to the Hebrews, the one wholly anonymous book in the New Testament and the one most likely to have a background in Alexandrian Judaism, the thought is developed by a reading of Psalm 95, a poem about the wilderness wanderings of Israel which ends, "Wherefore I swore in my wrath, they shall not enter my rest." The author invites us to read this last line in the light of another "rest" referred to in the Hebrew Scriptures, the "rest" of the Creator on the achievement of creation, symbolized and recalled in the observance of the Sabbath. If the testimony of created nature is that God rested from his works in satisfaction, are we not bound to think, the author asks, that "there remains a rest to be entered"? With wrath finally put away, must not the good of creation find its ultimate confirmation in the accomplishment of history? Reflection on the accomplishment of creation leads inevitably to reflection on the accomplishment of history.

From a different intellectual tradition, nurtured in Jewish prophecy, another figure of the first century known to us as John of Patmos follows a parallel train of thought. The universe, laid out in all its complex beauty and vitality before the Creator's throne, he sees and hears as a perpetually recurrent and repetitive performance of a hymn of praise. But his view of it is interrupted by a disturbing feature: in the hand of the Most High there is a scroll, sealed seven times. The sight reduces him to tears, as he confronts the very problem we have been confronting: How is it possible to know the goodness of God in the repetitions and recurrences of reality if we have no clue to the meaning of historical events? A good of nature could be conclusively good only for an ahistorical observer, if we can imagine such a thing. Everything that does not recur and repeat presents a threat to the sufficiency of the recurrent good. John then goes beyond the Alexandrian author in thinking that a positive overview of history is needed, not only to fulfill the promise of creation, but to rescue its apparent good from reduction to meaninglessness. This positive account cannot be read off creation, for there it is sealed against every attempt of intelligence to penetrate it. The only possible solution is a historical proclamation: "Weep not; lo, the Lion of the tribe of Judah, the Root of David, has conquered, so that he can open the scroll and its seven seals" (Rev. 5:5). Out of the history of Israel, John believes, the meaning of world history will emerge. But that will not happen straightforwardly: in a celebrated transformation of images, the prophet is told to look for a lion, and sees a slain lamb. To that Lamb the Ancient of Days entrusts the opening of history.

The question of the good of history arises from an insufficiency in the good of nature. If we are persuaded by Kant that without *some* historical good practical reason remains suspended in the air unfulfilled and unfulfillable, we shall conclude that the prospect of Ethics depends on the question of history, too. But in our third lecture we shall identify a third element, also liable to disappear, on which the recovery of Ethics depends. We describe it as the *acting person*.

THREE

The Missing Agent

In defending the reality of values against the legacy of Kant, Max Scheler found himself having to defend one value in particular, the supreme value of "the person." "The person"—"the most hidden of all phenomena," as he called it—stood in direct competition for supremacy with "history" and "community." He contended that "the being and acting of persons (collective as well as individual . . .) is the goal of community and history."* Kant had cast no doubts on the value of the person. Indeed, the occasional poetic florescences that add unexpected patches of color to the desert landscape of Kant's prose are, more often than not, in praise of "personality." But in a criticism that proved quite decisive, Scheler accused Kant of failing to understand the tendency of his own thought at this point. The respect for persons Kant extolled, he argued, was not directed to *real* persons at all, but to an impersonal principle of rational conduct.** The moral philosophy he had bequeathed the West was a philosophy of action, in which an agent was no more than "the logical subject" of an action. It was a form of naturalism

* Max Scheler, *Der Formalismus in der Ethik und die materiale Wertethik*, 400; Eng. 525. The reference to a goal of *history* is exceptional in Scheler, and undeveloped. But cf. 384; Eng. 370: "the sacred end immanent in history as a whole."
** Scheler, *Formalismus*, 384–86 ; Eng. 370–73.

that sought to explain the recurrent processes of action.* And that is how Kant's influence lay behind Scheler's other *bête noire*, the analytic psychology that was gaining ground at the end of the nineteenth century, a literature he read extensively. Viewing the life of the mind in terms of its patterns of experience, normal or pathological, he found no reference to personal subjects. The person who performed the activity or suffered the pathology had gone missing. Here, then, we meet the third vanishing element that has tended to cause Ethics to disappear into more reductive accounts of human action.

PERSONALISM

Scheler's ambition was to argue back from acts to real persons. His argument unfolds in two steps: First, since action is complex and extended over time, if we are to talk about it at all we must be able to talk about its relation to a continuous subject with a sustained practical rationality and purpose. Only so can we distinguish a course of action from a random sequence of occurrences. Second, the agent-person is recognized by an intuition that accompanies the recognition of purposeful action. We do not know ourselves as persons by introspection. The person is not the *Ich*, or the "self," the secret storehouse of psychological events and functions that Augustine discovered when he opened the door upon his inner life.** An inner self can never take responsibility for what it does. The person is the "I" who acts, and I know my-

---

* The self-conscious development of a reductive account of persons along these lines has of course been a consistent feature of English-speaking moral philosophy, as in Derek Parfit, *Reason and Persons* (Oxford: Clarendon, 1984).

** "Self" is much preferable to "I" as an English translation of the psychological *das Ich* in Scheler. The use of "I" is confined to the subject. If we are to employ a pronoun, it should be the "me," as in the French *le "moi."* "Ego," though used as a term of art in English-language psychology to convey *das Ich*, in popular speech contains overtones of an inflated or aggressive self-image.

self as "I" only by recognizing a series of events as actions I have performed. Other persons are recognized in the same way. This leads to a definition, restricted in scope but, Scheler believed, ontologically secure: *the person is the concrete, self-subsisting, and real unity of acts of different kinds.** Which leaves the word more or less equivalent to our English word "agent," a continuous subject of action through a series of acts.

This account of the person has one important implication: persons, like values, are entities known to practical, not to theoretical, reason. The person, Scheler claims, stands at the highest level in the order of values, and the "person of persons," God, stands at the very summit of that order. We would not be wrong, I think, to see in this a certain softening of Scheler's reservations about the coincidence of supreme value and supreme being. Admirers of Scheler such as Karol Wojtyła, later Pope John Paul II, found difficulty both with the breadth and with the narrowness of his definition. On the one hand, nothing is said to limit the "person" to the human species, so that the highest value is not a specifically human value. God and the angels count as persons, and the door is left open to the claims of some animals. All that matters is that we should be able to recognize a person through actions. Collective actors—states, churches, universities, political parties, and so on—are no less persons than are individual subjects. On the other hand, the reference to "acts" may seem to set the bar for personhood too high. At one unsettling moment, Scheler's distinction between the personal and the human seemed to be pushed to the point of conceding to ancient Roman law the right to deny children, slaves, and women personal status, since they could not act *suo jure*. Scheler did not mean to draw that conclusion; his point

---

* Scheler, *Formalismus*, 397–98; Eng. 382–84. Cf. 502; Eng. 482: "The person subsists as the concrete unity of the acts it performs, and only in the performance of them. It 'lives' (*er-lebt*) its being and life (*Leben*), including the 'life (*Erlebnisse*) of the mind,' so-called, and is never itself 'lived' (*gelebtes*) as being and life."

was simply the inadequacy of criteria based on species member-ship, though it could seem to leave the conventions and laws of any place and time uncomfortably free to determine the recog-nition of persons as it might choose. To argue that a child is *not* a person because there are things it cannot do, would be the same category mistake, in Scheler's view, as to argue that a child *must* be a person because it *can* do this or that. To treat personality as an attribute confirmed by performance, observed either by inspection or by introspection, is the basic mistake he wishes to identify. One might decide that a strange biped was a member of the human race by observing its capacity for calculation and memory, but one could not decide it was a *person* in that way. We *encounter* persons as we are caught up in happenings that simply have to be the acts of a practical intelligence. "It belongs to the essence of the person that it exists and lives only in the performance of intentional acts."* *Where*, in what species, in what classes of species, we shall find such acts of practical in-telligence, we just do not know in advance.

So neither is the claim for the supreme value of persons a claim for the value of the *capacity for agency*. Agency is the ab-stract name we give to an immanent power of action in concrete subjects. It is not the power that we must respect; it is the sub-ject of the power, the personal being that displays it. Powers can be enhanced or diminished. Personality is not an attribute one could enhance or diminish; it is the concreteness of acting being one can only encounter and admire. "Personalism" be-longs to a type of moral theory that prioritizes evaluative over deliberative judgments. Values frame the moral universe; they elicit admiration or detestation. The fact that some of them lie within our reach as ends of action is a secondary consideration.

* Scheler, *Formalismus*, 405; Eng. 390. A comparison with more recent English-language attempts to ground the status of persons on "incorrigible and immediate knowledge" of feelings and intentions would be rewarding but cannot be undertaken here. See, for example, Roger Scruton, *Sexual De-sire: A Philosophical Investigation* (London: Weidenfeld & Nicolson, 1986), 36–58.

The value of persons is not among those modest values that we may do something about, to realize them or enhance them. We cannot produce persons; we can only acknowledge them. The life and action of some persons may be flawed and defective, the life and action of others may be exemplary; in either case how we value what they *do* is secondary to how we value *them*. And if, in the wake of Kant, persons have gone missing from ethical theory, the reason, Scheler will have us understand, is that the recognition of *personal value* has gone missing. The subject and object of moral thought stand or fall together; the person valued and the person valuing are of one nature. When Ethics loses personal value from its center, it is reduced to the residual exercise of deliberating about ends and means of action—ends of no personal value, actions of no personal subject.

At such moments as this we become aware of the debt Scheler owed to the mainstream of Catholic Christianity, fed by the Gospels and Christian antiquity. For the source from which this idea entered Western culture was the teaching of Jesus of Nazareth about the "heart," the moral subject from which all explicit performances, good or evil, sprang. In the Hebrew tradition on which Jesus drew, "the heart" could mean simply the practical activity of the mind, the thinking that preceded the doing. But in Jesus's use, the heart is prior not only to the doing of outward acts but also to the thinking of them. It precedes inner and mental performances as well as outer and physical ones. Action—whether mental or physical—is expressive of an underlying personal reality, which is the final object of evaluative judgments. "Either make the tree good, and its fruit good; or make the tree bad, and its fruit bad; for the tree is known by its fruit" (Matt. 12:33). Yet Scheler goes further than this: the person is not merely the good or bad subject of good or bad activity; it is the *original* site of good and bad as such. For that stronger claim I have not found an explicit argument in Scheler, and I suspect that without a more developed concept of history, he could not form one. Implicitly, however, we may discern an appeal to Scotist ontology, assigning transcendence to the particular over the universal. The *form* of nature and the *unfolding* of time are made to focus concretely in personal encounters, where the transcendental conditions of existence converge in a real unity. The person has a form and a time, but cannot be reduced to its form and time. So on the person, ultimately, all our wonder is focused. There we gaze into the depths that lie behind and beyond the dimensions of the world that we know.

In asserting the ultimate value of the person, Scheler was driven to extend his disagreement with Kant to include what Kant had called *Gesinnung*. Here is one of those (unfortunately common) German words that make one despair of meaningful translation. Of the wide range of suggested English equivalents, some more plausible and some less, I have come after hesitation to favor "commitment." The argument in its favor is that it allows us to see Kant's position and Scheler's counterposition as rival answers to the same question, which is: If value resides ultimately in the person, but the moral value of one person differs from the moral value of the next, how do we name what it is that makes the difference between a "good" person and a "bad" person? "Commitment," prior to deliberation and action, is, according to both thinkers, the most original form of personal moral stance. Kant identifies it with the sense of duty, adherence to the demand of moral consistency. If it were tied to anything else, it would produce a "material" ethics based on empirical experience and reducible to consequentialism. To which Scheler objects that it denies commitment any material content, requiring of the moral agent no moral *discernment* of the real world at all. It cannot "orient the will upon an overriding moral value."* What was described under the name of commitment was simply an acquired discipline of self-consistency. And since the only alternative to consistency is inconsistency, Kant could not recognize bad commitments. For him, as for William Blake, it would seem that "if the fool would persist in

* Scheler, *Formalismus*, 113; Eng. 115.

his folly he would become wise."* He forgot, Scheler declares, that the devil is as systematic as God is.** Neither could Kant accommodate the sheer *variety* of commitments corresponding to the variety of values: not only are there "good" and "bad" commitments; there are vengeful, distrustful, adventurous, cautious, affectionate commitments, etc., etc. To justify the high claims made for it, commitment must involve the elementary discernment of real values and constitute an inchoate practical response to them.

Central to Scheler's view is the possibility of a *change* of commitment. A commitment is not a fate with which we are born; it is selected, exercised, developed, and transformed. From a defensive-aggressive attitude to the world I may come to assume a more trusting and open attitude. I may learn to view the world with more irony or more pity. Moral philosophy must make room somewhere for conversion. Conversion is a "voluntary" event, not brought about by simple act of will but (in a clear echo of Augustine) changing what we are *capable* of willing. Conversion is also a cognitive event, a change in how experience is understood, and so bound to the truth of experience as far as that can be established. Commitments change *as* we learn things and have new experiences, but they do not change *as a consequence* of learning things and having new experiences. The Christian teaching that conversion is a work of God's grace has a philosophical point of purchase. For Kant, as Scheler reads him, there can be no transformation of commitment, only the perennial tension between the ideal self and the actual self, eased to a certain degree by reasonable faith that moral effort is crowned with success. Where Scheler has learned from Augustine, Scheler's Kant has learned from Pelagius.

---

* William Blake, "'Proverbs of Hell' from *The Marriage of Heaven and Hell*," in *Poetical Works*, ed. John Sampson (Oxford: Oxford University Press, 1913), 250.
** Scheler, *Formalismus*, 20; Eng. 25.

The simplest way to sum up what is at stake here is to speak of a "self-transcendence" of the person. What Scheler feared in Kant's doctrine was an agent wholly self-enclosed, circling round its own sphere of rationality with no capacity to encounter or respond to a universe of values outside itself. Any morality worth the name must turn the self outward and engage it with the reality of the world. That turns Kant's ascetic program for Ethics on its head. Both thinkers made use of Jesus's teaching that "whoever would save his life will lose it; and whoever loses his life will save it." But where Kant thought it meant that the *sensuous nature* must be sacrificed to make way for the *rational will*, Scheler understood it to mean that the *will* must be sacrificed, to make way for the *evaluating person*. We cannot "will" the world of values into existence; it exists already, and on the highest values the will has no purchase at all. But the defeat of the will's pretension to *create* values sets us free to *encounter* them. And it is through encounter that we recognize the highest value in reality, ourselves as persons and others as persons. This recognition becomes, on Scheler's construction, the central formal test by which any Ethics is judged.

Kant famously had a difficulty at this point. In the *Grundlegung* he assumed he could make a seamless transition from the principle of rational self-consistency to respect for persons. The first formulation of the categorical imperative was "Act as if the maxim of your action were to become by your will a universal law of nature . . ."; the second was "So act that you use humanity, whether in your own person or in the person of any other, always at the same time as an end, never merely as a means."* Apparently he assumed that the first implied the second. But the first formulation can be obeyed—*must* be obeyed, in fact— without the agent's knowing that there exists any moral agent other than himself or herself. So this "other person" in the second formulation, where did it come from? Outright solipsism Kant disallowed, since the reality of the world was a datum of

* Immanuel Kant, *Grundlegung zur Metaphysik der Sitten*, AK 4:421, 429.

intuition; yet a perfectly real world does not have to include more than one real rational person. So in the *Critique of Practical Reason* there was a second, more carefully judged attempt to manage the transition from the universal law to the recognition of persons. The idea of personality, Kant says, awakens a respect directed by each person to his own moral nature; if the agent has "maintained humanity in its proper dignity," he has done so "in his own person." In the primary exposition of his theory, the so-called analytic, that is as far as Kant goes, but in the "dialectic," where he aims to bring the theory into harmony with a broader range of anthropological questions, he allows that "in the order of ends the human being (and with him every rational being) is an end in itself."* The context in which the other person, now described as a "human being," is recognized, is moral faith. The epistemological standing of the other person is effectively the same as that of God, whose role as creator and moral legislator cannot be "known" by reason directly, but is believed, because the ethics of the moral law requires that belief in support of its practical motivation. The other person is thus posited in faith, and posited in faith as human, that we may treat the end in itself, rational personality, encountered *in* ourselves as we obey the moral law, as *apart from* ourselves in a universe we trust as hospitable to morality.

In the received history of the category of "person" (and received histories, though often misleading, can sometimes be helpful), the use of the term as a category of moral anthropology is traced back to its use in the christological definitions that related the unitary "person" of Christ to the two "natures" of humanity and divinity. Boethius's definition, devised to explain

---

* Immanuel Kant, *Critique of Practical Reason*, 5:87f., 131. Charles Dickens gleefully parodies this doctrine, placing it on the lips of Mr. Pecksniff: "Mr. Pinch is an item in the vast total of humanity, my love; and we have a right, it is our duty, to expect in Mr. Pinch some development of those better qualities, the possession of which in our own persons inspires our humble self-respect." Charles Dickens, *The Life and Adventures of Martin Chuzzlewit* (London: Chapman & Hall, 1844), 13.

the formula of the Council of Chalcedon, declares that the person is *naturae rationabilis individua substantia,* the individual substance of rational nature.* The late Robert Spaemann distinguished two lines of questioning that grew out of this definition, both seeking to establish how we recognize persons. One attempted to clarify the qualities that distinguished a nature as "rational." The other attempted to understand what it meant for rational nature to be manifested in an "individual substance," and was concerned not with qualities but with *singularity and plurality,* with "persons" in the plural rather than "the person" in the singular.** One way of interpreting Kant's shift would be to see him abandoning the first of Spaemann's two lines of thought and attempting the second. In that case, the two major approaches of the present day to recognizing persons would both derive from him, the one from the *Grundlegung,* seeking objective criteria of personhood in rationality, and the other from the second *Critique.* Practical engagement, or moral faith, comes first, without supporting theoretical grounds. To recognize persons we must be *ready* to recognize them. And we will make ourselves ready, because it is essential to any and every rational practical undertaking that we should be ready. Skepticism about persons is possible, but it is paralyzing from a practical point of view. This is the line that Spaemann himself seeks to advance, and in so doing he follows Scheler's assertion that the intuitive recognition of persons is "underived." And as there is no prior rational criterion, so there is no privileged place for self-consciousness in discerning persons. We do not extrapolate the idea of the acting person from our experience of ourselves. We know ourselves as acting persons in the same way that we know others, by recognizing acts we have performed as

* Boethius, *Contra Eutychen* 3.
** Robert Spaemann, *Persons: The Difference between "Someone" and "Something,"* trans. Oliver O'Donovan (Oxford: Oxford University Press, 2006), 1.

we recognize acts that they have performed. The peremptory character of this epistemological foundation echoes throughout the twentieth century: we hear resonances of it in Barth, and even stronger resonances in Levinas.

Spaemann elaborated his point about recognition by exploring another notion already found in Scheler, that of a *community of persons*. To be a person is to stand in a distinctive transcendent relation to one's nature, in our case a human nature, a relation Spaemann describes as "having" that nature rather than simply "inhabiting" or "living" it.* We reflect upon our nature and consciously act to shape and interpret it. Whereas all "natures," all kinds of things, have particular instances (if there are cats, there is *this* cat; if there are rocks, there is *that* rock), persons are not just instances of a kind, "persons." The phrase "this cat," accompanied by a pointing gesture, refers to its object adequately; the phrase "this person" does not do so. To refer to a person adequately, one must use a name. And there is an appealing metaphor for the relations of persons that Spaemann may have found in Scheler but puts to his own uses: a person is a unique "place" within the universe of values. Places, too, as quasi-personal constructs, have proper names—a point of which Proust makes a great deal: "How much more individual was the character that places assumed from being designated by names, . . . proper names such as people have."** And as places are identified only ostensively, on a map where their position is plotted in relation to other places, so that St. Andrews is identified as east of Cupar, north of Anstruther, etc., so a person is identified in relation to other persons. If I ask, "Who am I?" it is not senseless to look for an answer by naming the significant others with whom my life is bound up. But there is a point at which the analogy of persons and places fails. Personal

---

* Spaemann, *Persons*, 29–33.
** Marcel Proust, *Swann's Way*, trans. C. K. Scott Moncrieff (London, 2020), 407.

names are used primarily not to *refer* to particular places in the universe of values but to *address* them, in the second person. Personal existence is known not by way of objective reference but by encounter, as we speak to another and are spoken to. Such was the thesis Scheler's friend Martin Buber propounded in *I and Thou.** And this brings us to the startling paradox of personality. A "nature" may have one instance in fact. We can imagine a world with just one mountain, one giant panda, even one human being, so long as there *could have been* more. But a *radically* individual being, a person, can only be known by other radical individuals. Either there are at least two of us, or there are none of us at all.

We can trace, then, a continuity of approach from Kant's moral faith to Buber's "I and Thou" and Scheler's "community of persons," each locating access to personal knowledge in personal encounter. In Scheler's and Buber's technologically innocent world, it was possible to stop at that point. But Spaemann, enmeshed in late twentieth-century struggles over bioethics, could hardly dismiss so lightly the descriptive task of plotting properties and conditions. It may be true that we know a person only as we meet one, but if we know a person only as we are disposed for such a meeting, must we not ask when and under what conditions it is imperative to be so disposed? In a world where we are blindly governed by technology, it can be urgently important to know when we may have to open our eyes. Someone who talks to a dog (not giving commands but offering information or encouragement or consolation) is treated as a genial soul; someone who talks to an African violet is thought slightly eccentric; neither is supposed to be wholly serious. It is viewed as a kind of game, possibly a useful game in managing dogs or making violets grow. But when a pig cries out at us from an advertisement for veganism to treat him as a "someone, not a something," or when we hear reports of porpoises circling around a human swimmer to ward off the

* Martin Buber, *I and Thou* (Edinburgh: T&T Clark, 1937).

attentions of a shark, the stakes become much higher. And how much higher again in the bitter generation-long struggle over the public failure to give legal protection to the human child in the womb!

So the question of criteria for persons, banished as some kind of category mistake, returns in a modified form. What kind of *correlation* could there be between the "person" whom we recognize absolutely, without criteria, and the "nature" that is supposed to support personal existence? Spaemann suggests that the only external indicator that could rationally dispose us to anticipate encountering a person is the natural species to which the supposed person belongs. Species of life differ in their characteristic features; some do, and others do not, present features we assume to be necessary underpinnings for personal existence. We must be candid about the purely hypothetical character of such assumptions. We are familiar with persons speaking to us out of complex clusters of cells called human bodies; nothing we know about the universe rules out such science-fiction ideas as persons speaking to us out of shafts of light—hardly more difficult to conceive, perhaps, than persons speaking off printed pages or electronic chips. Yet experience does not warrant our listening expectantly to every shaft of light that falls through our window. We must build on the experiences we have, and since our most commonly admitted experiences tell of one species of being, our own, that initiates personal communication, we must accept that that imposes a reasonable duty of *presuming* personality in all living members of the human species, regardless of what *actual* personal communication we may or may not have had with this one or that. More contested but long asserted experience also tells of personal communication in prayer with a supreme being not of our own nor of any other species. With other animal species we have no sustained experience of personal interaction, though there are instances, mainly with domestic animals, that offer suggestive analogies that should at least persuade us to behave toward them with some restraint and consideration. Maybe that situation will evolve. But whether it does or not, the principle will hold: species recognition, while not the *ground* on which personhood is recognized, is the necessary and sufficient *precondition* for readiness to recognize it. If we are open to recognize a person in one member of a species, we are open to recognize a person in all members of it. "All porpoises, for example," as Spaemann, with a flourish, concludes his book.*

PERSONS AND TIME

This serious and sustained attempt to establish the idea of the agent-person in the face of idealist constructions of Ethics has had some stubborn difficulties to face.

To speak of a person is to speak of a being that achieves concrete identity *as* he or she engages in communication with other persons. To speak *of* a person is to speak *as* a person *to* persons, to be actually engaged in interpersonal communication. The view of the person, then, is limited to certain exercises of *practical* reason. How does this limitation relate to the seemingly theoretical and comprehensive judgment that the person is the "highest" value? If we unpack that troublingly quantitative claim, it may mean that recognizing persons and being recognized as a person are the necessary condition for satisfying all other moral aspirations. But to that contention there are two grave difficulties, one subjective, one objective, both having to do with time. First, there is a misfit between the comprehensive scope of the claim and our fragmentary experiences of moral satisfaction. Whatever moral satisfaction we feel, we feel it to be provisional. We may judge that particular deeds and experiences were good, but we make that judgment against the background of moral aspirations still unfulfilled. I may regard something I did as a success, but I am not in a position to call *myself* a success. I cannot yet grasp myself, whole and entire, as a person. When I finally do so, how can I know whether I shall

---

* Spaemann, *Persons*, 248.

be, or ought to be, satisfied? I can measure the success of what was done against its effects so far, but not against its further effects in the future. How can I know whether the future will validate the provisional judgment that it was a success? Secondly, any given person (myself or another or a collective person) is no more, viewed objectively, than a passing moment in the vast time span of the universe. How can the person claim to be more than an epiphenomenon, a "logical subject" of acts that flickers momentarily and disappears?

Time is one factor that forces us to admit the truth of Augustine's famous observation, "I am a great question to myself."* Let us confront the difficulty posed by time with an alternative: either it *matters*, or it does *not* matter, that persons are swallowed up by time, that their histories are at best incomplete, at worst lost in a temporal expanse too vast for historical narration. The implication of saying that it *does* matter is that our actual recognition of persons is provisional, not categorical and definite. To be sure of a person, we must wait on what *becomes* of him or her. But if we make that admission, the claim for the unfounded and absolute character of personal recognition seems to fall to the ground. If, on the other hand, it does *not* matter, personal status becomes atemporal, independent of time. Scheler boldly grasped that nettle, speaking of persons as *zeitlos*, "timeless." ** Values are ontological categories; though subject to disclosure within history, they are unchanged by history. The wedge thus driven between personality and historicity seems quite as blunt as the dichotomy of persons and humans in Kant. If people can recognize our concrete personal value independently of what we have been or are becoming, and can therefore see us *as* persons whole and entire, so that no future acquaintance with us could add anything to the person they see, how can personal insight be relevant to our active conduct of ourselves in time, which is apparently the business of moral reasoning?

* Augustine, *Confessions* 10.33.
** Scheler, *Formalismus*, 527; Eng. 507.

The challenge posed to persons by time is given an added sharpness of focus by death. When we die, the communities of which we are a part survive us, though they are not themselves immortal. This threatens the equilibrium in which the person stands to the social whole. "Life goes on," we say, meaning that social, biological, and cultural life goes on. Personal life does *not* go on, not, at any rate, in this world. Much of the impetus behind Scheler's doctrine was political: he wanted to defend a liberal view of political entities as composed of individuals against the socialist and nationalist collectivisms that proliferated in early twentieth-century Germany. Though an individual finds scope for self-expression only in the service of a wider community, he argued, the community cannot itself be culturally and morally enriched unless it makes room for individuals capable of the fullest self-expression—not a difficult claim to justify by observation. But this argument goes no further than "the" individual, which is a *generic* category for a *kind* of human presence in the world, a presence that is infinitely replicable. It is a favorite rhetorical ploy of the politicians to speak of "real people's needs," as though in speaking of "real people" they were speaking of *particular individual* people. But "real" people, in the argot of the trade, are classes of people defined by the most general concerns and needs, usually by a sense of being economically stretched. *Particular* people interest the politicians only to the extent that they conform to the pattern of "real people" and are therefore "typical"—that is, replicable and capable of aggregation in large numbers. It is not a criticism of politicians that they aggregate particulars; aggregates are their special line. The criticism is simply that they pretend *not* to do so. Their "real people" is a class with no members, for no concrete person is describable solely as an instance of the class that has only these generalized and aggregated concerns. As a particular and concrete person, everyone is different. The person "is individual," we could say, rather than being "an" individual.

As soon as we replace "the individual" with particular concrete persons—let us say, my parents, who are not your parents—then the law of personal uniqueness decrees that as no person is replaceable by any other, so the death of my parents cannot be compensated for, or balanced out, by the life of yours. Nor are concrete personal relations replaceable: when my parents are removed by death, other personal relations may fill a gap in my emotional life, but they cannot re-create the relation I had *with my parents*. In this respect the law of persons is quite different from the law of living organisms, which replace one another on the surface of the earth in a very obvious way. Personality forbids any such replacement. If faith allows us to speak of a communion of saints involving the living and the dead, it does so by suspending the organic relation in which we stand to the dead and holding the dead to be in some important respect living. How, then, can the value of a person who has died be irreplaceable? It may be said (and the answer is not to be despised) that every person is *memorable*. We remember persons we have loved with fondness; we remain conscious of them, sometimes more clearly at a distance than at the time. Yet the memory of a personal relation is not itself a personal relation, for it is not reciprocated. Memory, even if untouched by time, which it cannot be, is no more than a tender and regretful form in which we acknowledge the loss and accept the biological inevitability of replacement. Guilt accompanies the survivor's memory, guilt at having profited, though only temporarily, from that logic. And the memory dies with the survivor or fades into the shadowy traditions of historical narrative. If we invest some dead, and we cannot invest many, with the dignity of being "eternally remembered," we must do so on some other basis than memory itself.

It must appear, then, that the person represented as the supreme value can only be grasped from an eschatological point of view. At the end of time we may be in a position to say that the relation of persons to persons was the highest value time afforded, and that the concrete value of each person, seen not from within the succession of times but in a comprehensive and synchronous view, remained immortally precious. The religions of the world have taught us to imagine such a point of view by expecting a last judgment of the dead "according to their works," an expectation anchored *both* in the concrete reality of persons *and* in the meaning of their collective history. If one thought more than any other has haunted the reflections of a postreligious twentieth century, it is surely that this imagination, useful though it may have been, could not be realized. "I should like to be judged," says a dying philosopher in one of Iris Murdoch's novels; "I would want to understand it all."* He aspires to the true philosophical point of view on himself. Yet those are the *opening* pages of the novel, and in the subsequent chapters he will be replaced by the novel's main characters. The philosophical point of view is perhaps all that is left to our culture of the faith with which belief once confronted death, expecting judgment with greater or lesser hope of mercy. Heidegger famously tried to reconstruct it on existential terms by advocating the "authenticity" of "living towards death." But that could be no more than a technique for forgetting our incompleteness, trying to view ourselves *as though* we were seen whole and entire by some Other. Even from a philosophical point of view, that train of thought must be suspect; it could be moral prudence, but it is hardly moral wisdom. It could make us more aware of possibilities in ourselves, but its one-sidedness could also foster narcissistic overscrupulousness. So it seemed an inevitable consequence for much mid-twentieth-century thought that nothing useful could be said about an "authenticity" that trades on a personal knowledge of ourselves we cannot have. Moral judgment should venture no further, then, than asking what anyone else would, or should, have decided in similar circumstances. Thus the loss of the eschatological point of view went hand in hand with the further elimination of the person.

Despite the brave effort at recovery, the person persisted in disappearing. But must the eschatological point of view, after

* Iris Murdoch, *Nuns and Soldiers* (London: Vintage Books, 1980), 67.

all, be reckoned as wholly lost? We have already observed that an end of history, if such a thing can be known at all, must be known on the basis of a *promise* extended in the present. Might the person, too, benefit from such a promise? Might knowledge of ourselves and other persons be a kind of anticipation of something truly personal to come? And as Scheler insisted that the reality of the person must be grasped intuitively, not inferred from data of inner or outer consciousness, might not that intuition be given intermittently at moments of heightened moral awareness? Perhaps disappearing and reappearing are part of what personal existence, like the study of Ethics itself, involves.

Conscience and the Confession of Sin

We have closed the preceding two lectures by pointing to religious beliefs and practices that shed light on the disappearances. In closing this one, let us take note of the *confession of sin*. By whatever means it may be formalized and ritualized, confession seeks a recovery of personal agency grounded on acknowledgment of what has been unsuccessful or misdirected in its exercise. This is paradoxical, in that sin, rather than achievement, is the basis on which recovery is sought. Achievements and accomplishments present no threat to our construction of our life histories, but sin forces us to confront the difficulty we have in owning them. To be "bound in sin" is to lose the capacity to imagine one's agency coherently. An attempt to account for what one has done becomes ineffective; it turns into an account of what one has suffered, from the malign agency of demons or of other people, or from the workings of a meaningless fate. *Homo activus* vanishes behind *homo queribundus*, man the complainer, who, whatever he may be, is not an agent-person.

In confessing our sins as *ours*, we trace the unity of the agency that connects us with them and discover ourselves to be not merely creatures of moods and stimuli (though we cannot stop being that) but continuously responsible agents who carry our deeds with us, even when we take a new and altered view of them. Admitting the category of "sin" in our account of ourselves, we acknowledge ownership, and preserve self-unity in the face of the threat that past deeds pose to it. Of course, when we search for the thread of agency, we may fail to find it. And if we fail to find it, our claim to have grasped it may be an empty boast. "I accept full responsibility" is another of those rhetorical postures by which politicians actually sidestep responsibility. Is the true self-acknowledgment sought by confession achievable, then? Religious instruction asks us to believe that it can be given us as a grace, and asked for in prayer.

The name "conscience" has traditionally been given to this position of grace where, encountering ourselves through the sins of our past, we may encounter God and be affirmed in our personal agency. There is a hornet's nest of interpretative problems surrounding the concept—philological as well as epistemological and ontological. Some have thought—and in that vague allegation I include a former false step of my own—that it would be better to do without speaking of conscience altogether. But conceptual confusion often points to complex and important experiences, which one cannot get by without talking about somehow. "Conscience" translates the Latin *conscientia*, also translated "consciousness." At one end of its semantic range *conscientia* is a general capacity to register experience and take note of the world: one recovers "consciousness" when emerging from an anesthetic. Further along the range it speaks of a marginal awareness *of oneself* that accompanies awareness of other things within the world. At the far end it is a distinctly *moral* awareness of oneself, a sense of the good and evil of one's own being and action. Most modern languages have broken *conscientia* up into two words—"consciousness" and "conscience," *Bewußtsein* and *Gewissen*—though the Romance languages have retained a single noun to cover the whole range (as with the French *conscience*), which they then qualify in various ways as *conscience morale* or *conscience de soi*. There is something to be learned from both linguistic strategies. Conscience is a form of consciousness, of cognition. But more specifically, it is cognition of oneself; and more specifically still, it is cognition of oneself as a *moral agent*, liable to incur approving or disapproving judgment.

For our present purposes, all that matters is to *notice* this self-knowledge, and how it situates the moral subject within three polar tensions, each of which sheds light on personal agency. First, there are both *permanent* and *occasional* experiences of conscience. We experience it as a moment of discovery, when we are "smitten" by conscience or "prompted" by it. And yet it is not like adding a new piece of information to our stock of knowledge; the moral truths that conscience calls to mind are truths we were well aware of, and that is part of what makes the experience appalling: we realize we have lost touch with ourselves in forgetting them. Second, conscience moves between *certainty* and *doubt*. The German *Gewissen* originally meant "certainty," but much experience of conscience is of cognitive irresolution and anxiety over what we cannot reach a judgment on. In a memorable phrase, Saint Paul described conscience as "conflicting thoughts [that] accuse or perhaps excuse" (Rom. 2:15), a perfect evocation of this doubtful and disoriented self-knowledge. The third polarity is between the *affective* and *cognitive* dimensions of conscience, or more precisely, between moral *self*-cognition and the moral cognition of the *outer world*. While conscience is a feeling, an experience of myself as I am, it is also a recognition that certain other things are as they are, irrespective of my feelings. *Vox conscientiae vox Dei*, the old saying went; while our moral view on the world is never other than a subjectively human one, it is not confined to recycling the immanent resources of the mind but is a means to put us in touch with things as God sees them.

Religious instruction invites us to enter the process of self-questioning that can help us sustain our personal agency. It offers us the hope that through its uncertainties we shall be led to moral clarity, not only about our deeds but about ourselves, so that we may be able to reclaim ourselves and act. That is the "good conscience" that the rite of baptism is said to be an appeal for (1 Pet. 3:21 ESV). The perpetually troubled conscience is necessarily a failed conscience, one that cannot attain the clarity of resolution sought. We are also invited to believe that this discipline, if seriously undertaken, is never solitary. Whatever the subjective limitations and constraints our conscience may suffer from, there is a voice of God to be heard, partially and provisionally but really and sufficiently, enough for personal agency to be getting along with.

FOUR

Creation and the Recovery of Reality

In the first three lectures we identified three threatened elements
of Ethics and pointed out how traditional religious disciplines
have served to protect them. In the remaining lectures we gather
some of the resources of theology to address these disappearing
features, beginning with the understanding of creation.

THE BLINDNESS OF NATURE

We took our departure from Kant's attempt to drive a wedge
between natural goods and a rational good of action, which
was his response to the early modern idea of nature, the discovery that all being can be viewed, and viewed fruitfully for
the purposes of some investigations, as a complex of interlock-
ing regularities of recurrent phenomena. In such a conception,
being, time, and the good are reduced to their lowest common
denominator, a form of regular recurrence that deprives each of
its distinctive character. The being of things loses the attribute
of concrete subsistence and disappears into replicable kinds of
phenomena. The time of things loses its eventfulness and becomes an extended display of regularity without novelty. That
useful German proverb *einmal ist keinmal* catches the point precisely: the being or event conforming to no law is, as it were, a
nonbeing and a nonevent, part of no objective knowledge or
happening. It sits on the sidelines of investigation as an anomaly
waiting for some law to be discovered that will make it repli-

cable, and so real. In nature's realm nothing happens that does not display conformity. Early modern nature is blind to the concrete and the new.

Nature is also blind to the good, which loses its moral sovereignty over evil. For in nature's realm good and evil appear together as complementary aspects of a circular process. If vegetables are good for animals as food, animals are good for bacteria as habitats, and bacteria are good for vegetables as environmental conditioners, we have described a circle of goods that we can turn into a circle of evils simply by traveling round it in the opposite direction: bacteria make animals die, animals are predators on vegetables, and vegetables limit the reproductive success of bacteria. The mutual interchangeability of goods and evils is the hallmark of the natural system. Nothing in nature tells us that animal health is more important than the reproductive success of a virus; it is more complex, certainly, but not "better" or "higher." There is no place on the circle of goods-alias-evils for *the* good, the good we ought to prefer.

Once there was a more genial concept of nature. It prevailed in the classical world, which was not blind to the concrete, the new, or the good. "Nature" was *phusis*, which is literally "birth." Its normativity was the irreversible direction of organic growth, from birth to maturity. "Nature" was not a steady state in which multiple organisms sustained each other within a balanced system by dying and circulating resources for each other's use, but the energy of life itself directed toward growth. Moral good consisted in conscious conformity to emergence and development of life. Blindness to being, time, and the good was not a feature of *phusis*; blindness, in the ancient view, belonged rather to *tuchē*, or chance.

When the early modern conception of nature entered our civilization, the older conception did not simply go away; it went, as it were, underground. The official histories of Western ideas, based on a canon of texts produced by intellectual elites that was influential upon later intellectual elites, underestimate the capacity of human civilizations to harbor conflicting outlooks. The older idea of nature retained a popular adherence alongside the newer scientific one. My Irish grandmother would have said of the inhabitants of an unfriendly neighborhood in her city of Cork that they had "no nature," and this value-rich use of the term would, I think, have been understood at once by Seneca. From time to time the older idea of nature has re-asserted itself, as even the official histories notice. It inspired Goethe, Wordsworth, and the early romantics, and has surfaced again in recent years in ecological and biotechnical debates, so that it seems less unusual today than it seemed a generation ago to hear it said that nature lays a basic moral claim upon us.

It has been asserted, in fact, by so usually insightful an ob-server as Gerald McKenny that the older idea of nature shapes some of my own writings on bioethics.* I am quite sorry to have to deny it, but so far as I can establish, I did not make use of this idea in my occasional discussions of biotechnical questions.** In putting the record straight, however, I do not want to lend tacit support to the view that the older concept of nature has nothing to contribute. Given the gravity of what is at stake in our debates about the ecology of the planet, it would be alto-gether too facile to fall back on the commonplaces of the official histories of Western ideas. Moral orientations depend upon the principle of consistency, that like cases require like conduct. So long as human beings consistently treat birth as an occasion of joy, fear and shun disease, and mourn premature death, they have sufficient grounds in practical reason for regarding certain natural events as inherently good or inherently evil. And this allows them to view acts or omissions that promote or prevent

---

* Gerald McKenny, *Biotechnology, Human Nature, and Christian Ethics* (Cambridge: Cambridge University Press, 2021). McKenny has in view my *Begotten or Made?* (1984; new ed., Landrum SC: Davenant, 2022), where I criticized the role of technological thinking in bioethics.

** I owe to Samuel Tranter, *Oliver O'Donovan's Moral Theology: Tensions and Triumphs* (London: T&T Clark, 2020), the reminder that in an essay of 1978 I said that nature and creation amounted to the same thing. By the time of *Begotten or Made?* I had learned better.

those natural events as *prima facie* morally good or evil, and to ask whether new types of biological intervention, such as artificial reproduction or ecological nonintervention that permits species deaths, are morally good or evil forms of practice. The normative language that lies closest to hand for a secular discussion of these questions is that of nature. While there are good reasons to look for a better language, the validity of the question does not depend on the adequacy of that category. It depends on the actual realities of life and death and the actual prospects of artificial life and species death. We can hardly require that these questions be put on hold while we gravely remind one another that normative concepts of nature were replaced by value-free ones somewhere between the thirteenth century and the seventeenth century.

Yet when all this has been granted, the idea of nature-as-birth does not afford a sufficiently stable underpinning for moral thinking about such questions. It adopts the perspective of the living organism itself, which has a spontaneous interest in living and continuing to live. It avoids the observer's view, which takes into account the place of death, decay, and recycling in the biological system. The observer's view, the view distinctive to modernity, cannot just be *avoided*. For scientific purposes, at least, the modern idea of nature is not just one idea on the table; it has set the agenda. It has brought with it an idea of conformity to natural laws that makes any talk of *moral* conformity sound like equivocation. We have seen how philosophy, faced with the observer's view, could not continue to think of itself as "natural philosophy." It needed to find a position beyond nature, in what Kant called "freedom," an initiative in excess of natural conformity. We have seen, too, how it needed to discover "history," the irreversible progressive logic of unique events. From these two needs arose the opposition between practical and theoretical rationality bequeathed by Kant to his successors. If we are to get behind that opposition and achieve a philosophical reintegration of nature, history, and freedom, we need strong additional reasons to believe that the ancient view of nature as growth is something more than a wishful projection of our specific or individual interests in staying alive. To justify a moral preference for life over death we need an authority from outside nature to support belief in the capacity of history to "fulfill" nature by decisively vindicating life. Without this, even the most farsighted ecological concerns will be bogged down by the irresistible facticity of our human impact on the earth, all the more strongly evident as we seek to "save" what we perceive ourselves as having compromised. The idea of living harmoniously with a nature of which we are part is as difficult to imagine today as it ever has been, and to give it substance we shall need to know more than Isaac Newton could teach us.

CREATION AS ORIGINAL COMPLEXITY

At this point theology has a contribution to make with the concept of creation, a theme of central importance to Jewish and Christian faith and with an obvious bearing on modern vacillations about nature. There have been periods in the history of theology when it did not seem so important to articulate the idea of creation as distinct from the classical idea of nature, so closely did the two appear to interlock. But at other times, and especially in recent decades, theologians have felt the need to describe with much greater care the logic of the assertion that the world is created. If nature offers no foundation for values or for obligations to life and the environment, that is because "nature" does not say everything that "creation" says. If a language of nature continued to have a place in theology, as it did, for example, in the work of Lubac and his followers, it had to be reinformed by the idea of creation. Bernd Wannenwetsch has written, "While there is legitimacy to appeals to nature in Christian moral thought in principle, this legitimacy exists only insofar as such appeals are not abstracted from the doctrine of creation in its fullness."*

* Bernd Wannenwetsch, "Creation and Ethics: On the Legitimacy and

The logic of creation is that *act* precedes *being*. "Creation" is a noun of action. As the late Christoph Schwöbel summed it up, "There is nothing 'given' for the creative act of God."* In the beginning was the divine act—the *Wohltat*, as Barth describes it in his magnificent account of the doctrine of creation.** In the hands of Barth's translators, *Wohltat*—no more easily translated than certain other German words—becomes "benefit," which throws too much weight on the *good effects* of God's deed. What it should point us to is the original *enactment* of good. Not a benefit *to* any one class of beneficiaries rather than another, not a benefit of any one distinct kind rather than another, but a good, and therefore beneficial simply and as such *by virtue of being done*. That act is the conferral of being on what is not by the One who is what he is. Let us refer, then, to God's "good deed," and make two introductory comments on it before exploring its implications in greater detail.

In original action, first of all, there is an original inseparability of being, good, and time. To "act," in the fullest sense, is to envisage a good as concretely determined at a point in time and to realize it. Though there are many things we call "acts" that do not correspond in every respect to that description—an "act of wanton destruction," for example, which does not spring from the determination of a good end, or an unsuccessful "act of policy" that does not realize the end as envisaged—yet we describe such acts as "failures." "Failure," in fact, is a term we reserve

---

Limitation of Appeals to 'Nature' in Christian Moral Reasoning," in *Within the Love of God: Essays on the Doctrine of God in Honour of Paul S. Fiddes*, ed. Anthony Clarke and Andrew Moore (Oxford: Oxford University Press, 2014), 199.

* Christoph Schwöbel, "Gott, die Schöpfung und die christliche Gemeinschaft," in *Gott in Beziehung: Studien zur Dogmatik* (Tübingen: Mohr Siebeck, 2002), 177: "Es gibt nichts Gegebenes für Gottes Kreativität, weil sie den Charakter des absoluten Gebens hat." At the time of these lectures, Professor Schwöbel's death was a painful recent memory among colleagues in St. Andrews.

** Karl Barth, *Church Dogmatics* III/1, *The Doctrine of Creation*, trans. G. W. Bromiley, T. F. Torrance, et al. (Edinburgh: T&T Clark, 1958).

specifically for defective acts, for the failure to act *well*, which includes acting *effectively*. In the original act, the act that makes possible all acts, the threefold cord of being, good, and time is unbroken. The act of creation is necessarily good by virtue of being real in itself and effective in time. Strictly speaking, the expression *Wohltat* is redundant, and *Tat* would have served by itself. But the redundancy is useful in drawing attention to the a priori connection between action and the good, and so serves to protect an adequate conception of act against an inadequate one. In Barth's use of *Wohltat* we hear an echo of Goethe's most quoted line, *Am Anfang war der Tat*, "In the beginning was the deed!," Faust's notorious correction to the opening words of St. John's Gospel. But Faust's own "deed" was a rebellion against reflection and worship, which was precisely what marked it as a failure. Unanchored and disoriented activity, supposedly typical of the modern subject, loses its relation to its being and its good, and hence to its time also. But if we assert action *in the beginning*, it must be action that founds the being, good, and time that are open to active participation, and therefore has these three dimensions of reality realized in itself.

In the second place, though this interpretation of creation in terms of being, time, and good is in a very obvious sense "metaphysical," it is also, in another and perhaps more important sense, antimetaphysical. "Metaphysics" is usually described as the attempt to *look behind* phenomena to observe basic structures of reality that give them form and significance, and on this account there will be many varieties of metaphysical thought, so that we may often understand "metaphysics" as no more than thought itself, engaged in its comprehensive ambition to organize experience. But it is easy to take a further step and perceive these "basic structures" as a kind of *explanation*. Explanations aim at simplifying, eliminating what is not essential to understanding. But what simplification could there possibly be of the universe of phenomena as a whole? The first requirement of a basic structure of the whole would be comprehensiveness, but if we follow the path of explanation, we eliminate what we take to be inessential. Thus metaphysics comes to look like another type of reduction. Reduction, as Husserl taught, is a technique of thinking indispensable to the pursuit of specialized knowledge but by the same token hostile to comprehensive knowledge. Reducing the many to the one; reducing being, time, and the good to regular occurrence; reducing reality to sensory experience—these are the sorts of explanatory ventures, typical of metaphysics, that have incurred suspicion, seeing them as a sophisticated attempt to ignore or forget, in the interests of explanatory economy, dimensions of reality we cannot imagine absent from experience. This suspicion is the steam that drove the twentieth-century project of "overcoming" metaphysics, a project easier to announce than to give direction to; but one thing it did suggest was a requirement to *account for* experiences suppressed or subordinated in large theoretical assumptions, so putting oneself on guard against the forgetfulness induced by successful explanations. There are obvious ways in which the modern conception of nature, led by the success of experimental method, is a "metaphysical" construction. What did it forget? As Kant knew, it forgot that the knowing mind was also the acting mind, and that a logic of regular occurrence in nature was not sufficient to guide action. It forgot, as Hegel knew, that the observable regularities of the natural world do not account for its history of unique events. It forgot, as Heidegger knew, that they do not account for the world we meet in existence, framed by unique and irreplaceable horizons. The piety of early modern Europe, too eager to find a theological endorsement of nature, misunderstood the doctrine of creation. "In the beginning God . . . ," it said, taking everything back to a single primitive reality. But what the ancient priestly narrators wrote was, "In the beginning God created the heavens and the earth" (Gen. 1:1), taking everything back to an original complexity bound together in a single act. Creation is not an explanation or a simplification of the complexities of experience. On the contrary, it affirms complexity as co-original with the world, involved in the first manifestation of being, time, and good.

Let us explore it, then, by examining the threefold cord of being, time, and the good, asking how each of the three forms a pair with each of the others in the original creative action.

a. First, there is the connection of being and time: the being of the world realized by God's dynamic act, as something happens in time.

The creation of the world, if we are to talk about it at all, must be talked about in narrative. Only secondarily and derivatively can we form doctrinal or theoretical propositions around it. Narrative is not governed by a need to simplify experience, to find a root cause or an underlying logic. It may sometimes be exploited in the service of theory to accomplish these things, but of its own bent it introduces time as foundational to all the relations that constitute the world. The words "in the beginning," with which the ancient Jewish narrative of creation opens, tell us that the being of the world is not eternal as God is eternal, but temporal. They point to the temporal *appearance* of being, and to the temporal continuity of all such appearances. They warn us against looking *behind* time to an ontological or teleological ground of experience, since time, and not being alone, is an essential condition of the world we inhabit. Barth was correct to insist first of all on the temporality of creation, resisting well-meant theological proposals to interpret it as an eternal dependence of secondary beings upon primary being.

Yet a narrative cannot narrate "the beginning" unless it also narrates what follows the beginning. Historians usually separate the narrative of any one event from the narratives of other events; they tell the story of the Union of Parliaments, let us say, without referring back to Marco Polo's journeys, and the story of Marco Polo's journeys without looking forward to the Union of Parliaments. But the narrative of the beginning is not separable. Its event is in an original relation to all other events. So in writing of the beginning of all natural things, the ancient narrators trace a sequence leading from Adam to Abraham and from Abraham to the world they know, connecting their own lives and their ancestors' lives to the original and essential enactment. Connected to its source, their time could no longer be thought of as no more than a refracting lens through which recurrent forms of being and the good were displayed in exemplary repetition. The narrative that unified history and being was a narrative of the action of God, and a world created is a world existing through and for action. Time is the "realization" of good and being, in the sense we have assigned to that word, not of making the unreal real but of making the real appear in its fullness. In antiquity Christians and Jews were troubled by objectors who asked why, if creation was very good, God did not make it earlier, so increasing the sum of good by extending the time of its duration. To which they replied, impatiently but satisfactorily, that since time itself was created, talk of time "earlier" than creation had no reference. If you ask when a beginning of some event should occur, the answer is given in terms of other events that set the conditions for it; if you ask when an absolute beginning should occur, "in the beginning" is the complete and total answer. Had they had more patience with their objectors, they might have pursued them a little further, pointing out that what scandalized them was not the *timing* of the beginning but the very *idea* of it. For a beginning must mean that the world is not transcendent over the action it contains. It subjects the whole being of the world to the time in which it has emerged, which must necessarily take the form not of empty time, in which either this or that event may happen or not happen, but of time already formed as an act.

The first creation narrative of the book of Genesis relates a series of enactments of being, each originating in its own temporal moment ("And God said, let there be . . ."), proceeding through the emergence of new being ("and it was so . . .") and culminating in reception of the good of being ("And God saw that it was good"). There is no suggestion that the series is governed by a causal or value-driven logic; good, being, and time are wholly present in each moment, no one of them assuming a generative priority over the others. The complexity of the originating act is displayed in two parallel narrative schemata of six days and eight acts, allowing no room for the idea of development or continuation. In the larger narrative of the book of Genesis, of course, there are developments and continuations. The narrative of the creative act is continued by the expulsion from the garden, the murder of Abel, the calling of Abraham, etc., but within the creation narrative itself there is no continuation. Everything is simply beginning. On the seventh day, the moment of reflective achievement, it reaches what we may think of as a kind of end of the beginning, which is also the beginning of ends, initiating the multiple forms of ending that the world will contain, archetypally presiding over ends of weeks, ends of lives, and the end of history itself.

"In the beginning" is a narrative formula deployed by the art of the narrator, as all references to first and last things must be. Narratives select their events, and their "beginnings" are chosen to construct the framework that defines the "story." In actual history beginnings are elusive. No event could be more concrete, it would seem, than the Union of the Parliaments of 1707, but where does the story begin? With the English Alien Act of 1705, the Scottish Act of Security of 1703, the initiative of William III in 1702, the death of Prince William of Gloucester in 1700? Or even with the Union of the Crowns in 1603, the Treaty of Perpetual Peace of 1502, or the wars of Scottish independence in the thirteenth and fourteenth centuries? We do not experience beginnings through the senses, nor do we hold images of beginnings in our minds. We intuit beginnings as horizons before which other things, set in temporal sequence, become intelligible to us. All thought of time, even of present time, is of this intuited character, stubbornly difficult to cast in empirical or imaginary terms. The "absolute beginning," the beginning of the world, is impossible to imagine, but simply for the same reasons in principle that any other beginning is difficult to imagine. It is certainly no more difficult to imagine than the pre-eternity of the world, which appears to be the only alternative. If we prefer the latter on the ground that time without horizons is more economical conceptually than time with horizons, our conclusion has merely been produced by the metaphor of the "horizon," since horizons in space are relative to the visual field of the observer. We may even suppose time to be "round," as the world is "round," with only, as John Donne said, "imagined corners"—but we would still gain nothing in *imaginative* perspicuity. All these difficulties are difficulties in thinking of original time, time that is not *our* time, commensurate with our being and at our disposal. Belief in creation, and therefore in beginnings, is an act of faith. But it is not a gratuitous act of faith. It is a posit we are invited to make in order to reap the conceptual benefits of thinking coherently *about the time of human action*, a time that cannot possibly dispense with either beginnings or endings. If action is to have a secure location in a history of the world, the world's temporal horizons are not dispensable either. Without them, talk of the world and talk of history fall apart, leaving speculative and practical reason to fall apart without a hold on one another, one engaged with a world constituted by the observable regularities of nature, the other with a history constituted by initiatives of action that can accomplish nothing in the world.*

b. In the second place, we consider the link between good and being. Set in the context of God's prior action, the good of our experience appears as the creation's *inner meaning*, the original direction given the world by God's good deed and disclosed through each event that happens within it.

In ancient myths of origin, of which it is often supposed that the Genesis creation narratives were intended as a critique, the relation of being and the good was uncertain and contested. There were myths presenting the original opposition of the two, as in the slaying of the primeval dragon, where moral form had to be imposed upon chaotic being and the good was a late-coming phenomenon in time, necessarily involving violence.

---

* This unnerving state of mind, I may be allowed to observe, is that inhabited by the religious characters in Iris Murdoch's novels, and probably by the author herself.

There were also myths of a primeval golden age, an original harmony of good and being disrupted by the incursion of time and its events. In the one myth good was *to be made*; in the other it was *to be lost*. And though we may sometimes need to say either of these things about particular goods, there is, as the Hebrew creation narrative presents it, a more fundamental assertion to be made about the good: neither to be made nor to be lost, it is real and present, given once for all in the enactment of being in time.

In the first lecture we approached the unity of being and good by way of the ontological status of the good. The creation narrative approaches the same point from the other end, by way of the moral status of the world's being. At each stage the enactment of being in time comes to rest in a reflection on the inherent good of being. "God saw that it was good" interprets each dimension of being as it appears, while the climax of the narrative sums up the complex whole as "very good" (Gen. 1:31). We suggested initially the thesis that "the good is given as being is given." Now we may invert the proposition, to say that "being is given as the good is given."

The phrase "is given," used commonly enough as a shorthand for "is present to experience," may carry little ontological, moral, or even temporal weight. Anything we experience—a triangular shape, a musical phrase, a logical entailment, or an earthquake—may be "given" in that loose sense. But once we speak of *the good* as "given," the expression inevitably acquires a stronger force. For we conceive the good as teleological, constituting an end or a satisfaction. That does not mean that everything given as good is consciously intended. Teleology may be thought of as an analogy: goods may be thought of as *like* ends, without being *instances* of ends that agents actually propose for themselves and take satisfaction in. In saying that being and good are given together, we may mean no more than that the world is universally good in the way that particular parts of it are good, such as the fruitfulness of trees or the beauty of the sun reflected upon waves. If these things please us, we recognize a certain affinity between our experience of them and our experience of ends we propose for ourselves; we may even travel to the seaside *in order to see* the sun on the waves, and so make an intended good out of a natural good. Yet the analogy need not end there but deserves to be explored further. If we are to enjoy goods, and to appreciate reflectively what we enjoy, we need to learn to *position ourselves* in a certain way toward them. Enjoyment is not automatic; it can be blocked by something within us. And the way we position ourselves is as recipients and beneficiaries. We find that enjoying a good is very like being the object of someone's kindly attention. It has an implicitly dialogical character; we feel addressed, affirmed, invited to respond. A businessman once wrote, reflecting on the success of his enterprise, "If I believed in God, I would say 'Thank you!'" As well as showing a creditable philosophical scrupulousness about *not* engaging in loose and indeterminate talk of gratitude without meaning it, the observation has a certain pathos, as of one wishing to rejoice in good fortune but lacking the conceptual repertoire for doing so. In his moment of satisfaction he finds that he had an expectation that remains unfulfilled: he hoped, despite his skepticism, that the good desired and achieved might have been a *communication* from someone.* The immediate expression of an intentionally focused joy is thanksgiving. And if we refuse the implications of thanksgiving, we have first to teach ourselves to *disown* our immediate joy, to see through it and to disembarrass ourselves of its spontaneous associations. We may train ourselves not to be spontaneously joyful, and yet it is painfully deflating to have to do so. Those versed in the language of phenomena like to distinguish "the given" from "the gift," the minimum on which we presume from the maximum to which we may look forward. But to what *may* we look forward, if not to receiving a good as an intentional communication?

* For a fuller elaboration, see my *Entering into Rest*, Ethics as Theology 3 (Grand Rapids: Eerdmans, 2017), 45–71.

We reach a proposal, then, that is surely worth the lumbering journey it has taken us to reach: the idea of the good is bound up with the intuition of a *communication*. Nothing is "good" for us unless it is addressed to us—not necessarily to a particular "me," but to an "us" I can identify with—the human race, the world of the spirit, the health of the planet, or whatever. And as the language of "gift" very easily dissolves into a minimal language of "the given," so the language of "goods" can easily dissolve into a minimal language of subjective demand, "wants." I once preached on the text "there is none good but God alone," and an elderly member of the congregation capable of reflective thought protested afterward that it had never occurred to him to think that there *was* such a thing as the good. It did not need to occur to him, so long as his ambitions were satisfied by demanding whatever it was he wanted. This is the logical inference from Kant's famous opening sentence of the *Grundlegung*, claiming that there is nothing *truly* good except a good *will*. For Kant it remained a question, at least, how a "will" might be "good," but the initial move had already destroyed the thought that the good might include, by analogy, other kinds of good—events, actions, agents, and so on—all of which we might welcome without first having had to will them, given to us as communications opening our eyes to new and wonderful things.

If we think of an original good, we think of a form received as a "gift," capable of evoking thankful response, within the very occurrence of the world itself. A recurrent form of nature requires no acceptance and invites no gratitude. Natural form is normative only in the sense that any logical idea is normative, namely, as an organization of experience. We are free to be disinterested in an ontological form, for human existence is our primary interest, and if the form is not addressed to us or anybody, it does not constitute a reason for us to notice it. But if a perennial form is also a communication, we can recognize, even in the regularities and predictabilities of the natural world, a gift on which the good of our existence depends. And that is a substantive reason for *free conformity* to the form as given, a better foundation for ecological concern than any that we normally hear. Once we have grounds to relate our knowledge of being to the conditions of our existence, then we can accept that the good of being is necessarily also good *for us*.* Nature acquires an evangelical content, not natural to it, bearing the promise of an existence in harmony with being. Thus the concept of creation forges a link between reality and moral existence in a world fitted to our agency.

In our first lecture we pointed to the practice of worship as a way of receiving the good. Calvin wrote that "although our mind cannot conceive of God without rendering some worship to him, it will not be sufficient simply to hold that he is the only being whom all ought to worship and adore, unless we are also persuaded that he is the fount of all goods, and that we must seek everything in him."** We note the admirable delicacy with which God as fount of "all goods" is distinguished from his being *our* good. Talk of goods is not immediately self-referential. Yet if we learn to "seek everything in him," the fount of all goods becomes the fountain of our goods, too. It is possible in principle to wonder at, even admire, forms of good that present themselves as bad for us. The natural world may confront us with "the sublime," evoking a shiver of horror at its indifference to human values. Only a true scientist could experience real delight in the coronavirus, with its amazing capacity to evolve and adapt its attack on human organisms. But for wonder at the world to become worship or moral regard, there must be an element of welcome as to something offered, whether or not the worshiper stands *particularly* to benefit from it. The communication of a good is essential to its recognition as good.

It may be a necessary presupposition of the train of thought we have followed so far that God is to be conceived as the

---

* Cf. my observations in *Resurrection and Moral Order: An Outline for Evangelical Ethics* (Grand Rapids: Eerdmans, 1994), 249–50.

** John Calvin, *Institutes of Christian Religion* (1559) 1.2.1.

original good. But our train of thought did not begin with the original good; it began with the original *action*, which implies good as bound up in being and time. As the psalm (119:68, author's translation) declares, "Thou art good, o Lord, and doest good." Moral experience is not simply the experience of gratitude and wonder at the good of being; it is the experience of being acted on and made active, occupying a place within the web of created goods that is fit for agency. And so it is that we derive our representations of the good as *normative* formulations, as ideals, as laws, as goals, and so on, in relation to which we regulate our conduct. Within the narrative of creation the normative character of the whole, its "holiness," is presented as the completion, the reflective achievement of the seventh day. It is because creation is a finished work, an order of things complete and entire, that it affords direction and sets bounds to action. Good is the real completion of being in time, yet it is open to further realization in reflection and response. These two aspects—completion and opening—must both be present in any comprehensive doctrine of creation.

c. It remains to say something about the third pairing, that between time and the good. The idea of time is the idea of a kind of extension and continuity in appearance. It may sometimes be represented as no more than an empty framework, or "container," of successive appearances, in which case time fulfills the role it is given within the modern idea of nature, that of a refracting lens through which being and the good in their recurrent patterns are laid out to view.* But there is an alternative. As seen in the light of creation as God's act, time is the form in which being and the good are given originally. In which case we must be able to speak of a *fulfillment of time*, just as we speak of a fulfillment of being and of good; there is an ontological and axiological plenitude that is realized essentially in time. Christoph

* The decisive theological criticism of the "container" view of time was made a generation ago by T. F. Torrance, *Space, Time, and Incarnation* (Oxford: Oxford University Press, 1969).

Schwöbel was among those who reminded us of "the promise of an eschatological future of creation."* Only in this way can time be understood as "history," a term which fills the idea of time with ontological and axiological weight. Present in reality, a gift once given on which there is no going back, the good still fills time and receives its fulfillment through time. And here we may rehabilitate, in its proper place, the moral "ought," which is constituted by measuring the future horizon of action against the reality of the good. "Ought" is a word that can be uttered with full definition and clarity only at the conclusion of a process of reflection and deliberation, in which the correlation of real goods with timely opportunities has come to focus upon a definite course of action still held open for us.

As we think of time as history, we think of it as having "beginnings." For beginnings belong together with continuations and ends as three aspects of historical form that cannot be separated. A beginning begins nothing unless there is a continuation; a continuation continues nothing unless there has been a beginning. If we say, "first there were gases, and then there were solids," we are not narrating history. For what we say contains no beginning, no continuation, and no end; it contains merely a sequence of appearances. But if we say, "out of the gases there emerged solids," we are on firm narrative ground, representing the gases as the beginning of the solids and the solids as the continuation of the gases. To make good our right to occupy that ground we must show how the gases contained the promise of solids and how the appearance of solids confirmed the direction indicated by the gases. The direction is not the beginning; it is a reference *from* the beginning *to* what follows the beginning, a promise proleptically present together with the beginning. And that is what is meant by an "end," in the fullest sense of that word. An end is not the same thing as a continuation; it is the measure by which a continuity is proved,

* Christof Schwöbel, "Theologie der Schöpfung im Dialog zwischen Naturwissenschaften und Dogmatik," in *Gott in Beziehung*, 144.

the substance of the promise that directs the continuation. So our grasp of the coherence of history is always proleptic, reaching beyond evidences, and our pursuit of historical knowledge characteristically takes the form of question and answer: What have we done? To what will it lead? Time as history is time encountered as a *direction* in the question and answer of the world's appearances, an ordering before and after that displays the intelligibility of time.

As we said about beginnings, so we must say about continuations and ends: they are not empirically grasped, but intuitively; they are horizons that make our experience intelligible to us. Submerged as our consciousness is in the flow of time, we find ourselves forced to employ these categories to understand sequential experience. To give form to our own small-scale endeavors we are committed to beginnings, continuations, and ends, and so, as we expand our horizon to the wider context of living and acting, we meet the questions of "absolute" beginnings and ends. There is no real line of demarcation separating our small-scale endeavors from the large-scale endeavor of life and action, nor the large-scale endeavor from the absolute horizon of time. A paradigm experience, common to the earliest explorations of the child and the broadest explorations of the human race, is the experience of *learning*. In learning we acquire the knowledge of something we did not know, and we acquire it by the means of something that we did know. Learning is fitting new knowledge into the framework of old knowledge. Coming to know something, we know more clearly what it is that we *did* not know and *needed* to know in order to complete the knowledge we had, and we also know more clearly what it is that we *still do* not know and *need* to know to continue the direction in which our knowledge has grown. Knowledge, in fact, is the paradigm case of finding ourselves willy-nilly in a directional movement, framed by beginnings and completions. The modern concept of nature, by making an absolute formal opposition between the reality known and the knowing observer, permits the observer to learn, and so to develop in time, but it does not permit the known reality to learn or develop in time. Time is thus abstracted from the world that is learned as a perspective unique to the learner. If that formal opposition is maintained stubbornly, it can only be at huge cognitive cost, as the twentieth-century development of the sciences increasingly recognized. Eminently more fruitful for knowledge is the recognition that new knowledge of reality implies new reality, that the world changes as it is known, since knowledge and its time belong within, not outside, the world. If the knowledge of the universe is, in some sense, a human vocation, there must be a corresponding vocation of the universe to be known.

In traditional doctrinal formulations, belief in creation is accompanied by belief in the continuing divine work, which divides in Christian thought into two strands, "providence" and "salvation": the doctrine of providence essentially conservative, treating the original gift as the historically continuing form of reality; the doctrine of salvation essentially renovative, anticipating the end of history. Human action arises in between these two poles of the continuing divine work. The possibility of the new is essential to the concept of action, as Hannah Arendt emphasized.* The archetypal form of history is expressed as Israel crossing the Jordan is told, "You have not passed this way before!" (Josh. 3:4). Yet the new does not *dissolve* the regularities of the form of reality given in creation. It opens up a future of the form as given. Barth was correct to see that it was by drawing out the implications of history that the ancient Jewish account of the world's origins acquired its distinctiveness. It presented a relation of form and event other than as an opposition. The pains of history are the pains of time in affirming and fulfilling the original gift (Rom. 8:19–23). The form of being assumes a historical dimension as it reveals the being and goodness of the Creator, who confirms his original gift by sustaining and renewing it.

---

* Cf. Hannah Arendt, *The Human Condition* (Chicago: University of Chicago Press, 1958), 175–81.

Here I must qualify (without entirely repenting) the severe treatment I gave in *Resurrection and Moral Order* to the idea of "continuous creation."* The conception I had to resist was that of an *incomplete* creation, a creation without integrity as a definite act, reduced to ongoing process and conferring no form on the world. I hoped to defend, in the first place, the conspicuous good of a creation order, necessary to the intelligibility of history and so to moral thought, and in the second, the conspicuous good of salvation as the fulfillment of that order. In the face of a theology that blandly identified itself by the name "process," such truths needed a defense. I may beg indulgence, then, for the sweeping way I dismissed the expression, for which there is a correct use. If we understand "creation" as a concrete noun referring to what God *has done*, not as a noun of activity referring to what God *goes on doing*, to say that it is "continuous" is simply to say that the created order is given a historical extension, sustained through time. But God's sustaining work cannot be understood without reference to his accomplished work; the two are distinct, but the second work presupposes and confirms the first. World history under God's direction is the history *of the world*, as formed and presupposed. If it were not so, there would be nothing to distinguish "history" from bare temporal succession or regular occurrence. History thus embodies the tension between unfolding novelty and the perennial form of things. The two ideas are correlative and mutually supportive, each liable to collapse without the other. A history consisting wholly of novelties, on the one hand, would be no history at all, since nothing is begun unless it binds the future to continue it; a history that led to no fulfillment, on the other hand, would not be a history, but a larger-scale nature.

---

* O'Donovan, *Resurrection and Moral Order* (Nottingham: IVP, 1986), 61, and (Grand Rapids: Eerdmans, 1994), 56. I had, no doubt, been instructed by Barth's *Church Dogmatics* III/3 (Edinburgh: T&T Clark, 1960), §49, p. 68: "We cannot say that he continues to create it. That is unnecessary, for it has already been created, and created well." Yet Barth also found a good use for the phrase *creatio continua*.

Origen got into trouble for looking too coolly at the *reductio ad absurdum* that turned history itself into natural repetition, so that new worlds (only rhetorically "new," of course) retrace the fall and restoration of the old, *ad infinitum.** The church was rightly shocked at the idea but was probably wrong to think that Origen took it seriously. Inferential logic, such as belongs to the study of nature and rests on the premise that all is ultimately repetition, cannot yield a knowledge of history.

Since knowledge of beginnings and ends is intuitive, "given with" our experience of time as history, any discovery we make of the meaning of time can be made only *from* history. Only in the light of what actually happens does time become intelligible. That order of discovery applies to any knowledge we may claim of the absolute beginning or end of history. It is not that we know creation first and conclude from it that history has a meaning, though that train of thought may be valid in certain contexts, as in a focused apologetic argument, for instance, or in the course of faith's search for self-understanding. But when Barth proposed, as the architecture of his interpretation of creation, that "the covenant" (i.e., the relation of God and man) was the "inner meaning" of creation, and creation the "outer basis" of the covenant, he intended to say that creation, if left to rest wholly on its own bottom, could never be more than a speculation. Its claim to a place in the knowledge of reality is that God has disclosed himself as active in history. The inverse is also true: history as a meaningful and purposive theater of action and life proves illusory if it is not framed with the horizons of a beginning and an end. And so together with himself God discloses the horizons that give history form, the initial gift of creation and his own ultimate reign.

THE WILL OF GOD

Up to this point we have spoken of divine *act*, implying the will to perform the act, and we have spoken of the divine *direction*

---

* Origen, *De principiis* 2.3 (Koetschau fragment 19).

of history, implying the will to bring history to its end, but we have made no explicit reference to the "will of God" as such. By approaching God's will in this roundabout way we have ensured, at least, that it has a concrete reference, too often lacking in the discussion of the topic. Everything that God wills, God does. If we ignore that and start looking for an anterior divine will that is *not* disclosed in God's moral direction of history, we encounter many problems in theology and ethics and are led down many false trails.

Yet it is inseparable from the very idea of God that he is "before" all things. To think of creation as God's act, we must think of God as an agent transcending his act, God in his "aseity" and "perfections"—a theme to which the late John Webster returned with great effect.* Does that expose the theologian to the charge of wallowing in metaphysics? Not if it is done prudently and comprehensively, imposing no preselection of worldly analogies that are supposed to illuminate the divine being more than others. But if we seize upon the *act of will* as an analogy uniquely capable of disclosing God's aseity, then we impose an arbitrary metaphysical preference on our thought of God. If voluntary decision and unconstrained freedom appear more fundamental than being, goodness, reason, or whatever else we properly attribute to God, we have let ourselves be guided by what we find most impressive in ourselves. We reveal the kind of God we ourselves would like to be. It is often said that modern voluntarism took the medieval idea of God as absolute will and transferred it to divinized man, which is true enough. But it is also true that the voluntarist divinity that came to expression first in medieval Augustinianism was *already* an idolatrous projection of the human ambition to be unconstrained.

But abuse does not invalidate use, and there is an important place for speaking about God's will. To know that God's deed is

---

* John Webster, "Life in and of Himself," in *God without Measure: Working Papers in Christian Theology*, vol. 1, *God and the Works of God* (London: T&T Clark, 2015), 13–28.

the concrete expression of his *will* is to know that the universe of being and goodness has a purposeful projection in time, a history to be fulfilled. The will of God manifest in creation is the vantage point from which the moral meaning of history comes into view, formed within the horizons of gift and fulfillment. It is not, of course, that Ethics can claim any knowledge of its own of the historical facts of God's dealings with the human race. No moral reasoning could prove or disprove the incarnation or the resurrection, nor even such a highly moralized event as the Babylonian exile of the Kingdom of Judah. Nor can moral reasoning declare, on the basis of historical accounts, what the meaning of such events must be. To narrate the events of the past as revealing a meaning in the will of God is the work of prophets, not of moralists. What moral reason can do, however, is to recognize the shape of a purposefully formed history when it is shown one. In the prophetic narrative of history it can recognize the purpose and the promise it anyway had to assume. Which is one supporting reason for the suggestion I threw out in the first lecture, that nowhere more clearly than in Ethics do we see what a "natural theology" may be.

Such a history requires action of us. We must pass beyond awestruck admiration of the blessings of creation to the tasks of practical reason. The concept of the will of God presents us with a ground for the category of *law*, the normative direction given to practical reason in history. This is the theme to which we turn in the next lecture.

Law and the Recovery of History

It may count as a commonplace of the theological tradition, especially in Protestantism where the contrast of law and gospel is more sharply made, that law is essentially timeless and ahistorical. Let us begin by demolishing that commonplace, calling in evidence the most wholly serious attempt there has ever been to understand history as law and law as history.

DEUTERONOMY

Somewhere toward the end of the seventh or the beginning of the sixth century BC, the age of the legendary foundation of Rome and the founding legislators of the city-states of Greece and Ionia, a remarkable document was composed to centralize and codify law within the small kingdom of Judah-Israel. In all probability it was part of the ambitious attempt of Josiah of Judah to reunify and reorganize Israel in the face of the military expansion of the Mesopotamian empires. The political hopes of that initiative were quickly snuffed out, but the longer-term impact of the ideas promoted in the book we know as "Deuteronomy," with its forceful Hebrew prose-style, elaborate, repetitive, rhetorical, and with articulate narrative resources, was immeasurable. It is no exaggeration to find in it the beginnings of jurisprudence and political theory, two intellectual enterprises it is hard to imagine the world being without. Its most innovatory claims would later come to seem commonplace:

that the essence of a national political identity was a unitary law embracing religion, government, family, business, and common life within a unified whole; that this unitary law depended upon monotheistic religion and universal legal education, through which God is "near" a people and ready to be "called on"; that while law must be reproduced and disseminated widely through tradition and education, it also needs a definitely identified authoritative text, to offset the legal corruptions traditional transmission tends to introduce; and that continued adherence to this single authoritative source required republication, exhortation, interpretation, and reapplication to new challenges and experiences. The form of Deuteronomy, accordingly, is that of an extended introduction and commentary on a short code of laws, evidently much older, to which great respect is paid. But that respect is matched by considerable freedom in elaboration and application: laws are introduced from other sources to supplement the code's provisions; new ones are added, especially to provide for a structure of administration and government. An authoritative interpretative tradition is defined, expounding sometimes archaic laws in line with clear administrative and hermeneutic principles.

Law is a norm; it has authority over our immediate conduct. The absolute authority of law, we suppose, is expressed in a present imperative, without past or future. With the passage of time the normative purchase of law is loosened, so that past law comes to be out of date. Deuteronomy intends to overcome these assumptions. There is a past event, it claims, that is decisively authoritative for the present and for all possible presents. When YHWH, having delivered Israel from Egypt, disclosed his will for their common life on Mount Horeb, all subsequent times were commanded. In that very act the detailed regulations for a settled civilization in the promised land were communicated to Moses for later elaboration and development. That one act of lawgiving revealed the moral meaning of later ages, including that in which Deuteronomy was published. It is law that makes time "history." Considered as "history," time is not an ever-rolling stream; it is a divine purpose shaped to an end. Reflection on this remarkable legal text requires us to engage with its strong thesis: *law is an implication of history; history is the fulfillment of law.*

The meaning of the first clause, that law is an implication of history, is not reduced to the trivial claim that the consciousness of law arrived on the scene at a certain point in history, though that is true; it means that law arises *from and within* history, as the form that history must take if there is to be such a thing as history, and not merely one thing after another. Law is the product of collaborative acts and practices; it directs all human acts and practices to a definite cultural end. In a sense that need not be prejudicial, Deuteronomy is a "historicist" text, finding its whole framework of meaning in history and the making of history, even to the point of ignoring the primal act of creation. The divine work was an evocation of history, eliciting in the midst of the nations an unprecedented and exemplary phenomenon, a law-governed monotheistic civilization. But can we imagine a morally characterized historical phenomenon without a narrative of free divine action? The concept of time itself is too weak to support one, the concept of human purpose too immanent in the circularities of nature. If the authority of law must reside in a particular history, it must be a history of disclosure—either a divine revelation, such as Deuteronomy recounts about Mount Horeb, or a self-revelation of the human will to bind itself in self-made rules for community. Of that second, positivist version of the revelation of law, I shall say no more than has often been said, and well: it subverts the idea of law in just the same way that positivist historicism subverts the idea of history, by making do without an end that makes sense of historical change. Law then rests on the decrees of established power, distinguished from them only by its relative complexity, its long established practice, and the formal mechanisms of its adoption. But the difference between moral authority and the fact of established power is a priori, constitutive of the idea of law itself. We shall confine ourselves, then, to the law that inherently claims moral authority, the law that asks to be obeyed because we know we ought to obey it. That law is not confined to institutions—states, voluntary organizations, and the like—but neither does it exclude them. Law is whatever presents coherent directive principles for life and action with moral authority *prior* to the decisions and judgments of those who publish it and obey it.

The second clause in our thesis, that *history is a fulfillment of law*, draws attention to how the historical emergence of law relates to the created goods we encounter. There can be no practical principles, we have argued, that are not derived from real goods of creation and providence. But practical principles are not given immediately with the goods of creation and providence. Constraints laid on the exercise of agency, duties and prohibitions conferred on different classes of people in different circumstances—none of these are immediately present in the world as we admire it and give thanks for it. Law appears in the world as an instrument of cultural development; it is "downstream" from creation. Adam's primitive observations of the world will have noted many forms of good but no laws for dealing with them; in naming the living creatures, he did not at once divide them into those that might and might not be eaten. The first command, a fruit that should not be eaten, arose with the first cultural task, preparation of food. Yet its authority was not independent of its setting in the new-made world where Adam learned to admire the good. It was a *mediation* of created goods in practice, imposing its authority as a framework of practical thought.

This does not make law a purely reactive phenomenon. For the command introduced an element of self-consciousness constitutive of the human relation to the Creator, subject to his voice and his call. Not simply *inferred* from created order, the command is a distinct step, a vocation that draws Adam out of natural immediacy into historical responsibility. As an anthropological reality law preceded guilt, Saint Paul argued, probably following a line of rabbinic reflection. The "death (that) reigned from Adam to Moses," an anomic guilt without moral definition, was "not like the transgression of Adam," which had been incurred in relation to direct command (Rom. 5:14). If the law that came through Moses gave definitive shape to that amorphous guilt, it was also a step to overcoming guilt. The human vocation from barbarism to civilization is an important background theme for Deuteronomy; there is a universal human destiny, pursued by law, of which Israel is to be the pioneer, a vocation to law-governed life as the fulfillment of created human life. But to know that much we need to be told more than the terms of human creation; we need to be told the historical form of God's dealings with humankind. Law is given to Israel through Israel's special history.

We shall, of course, immediately wish to add: to China through China's special history, to Rome through Rome's special history, and so on. And that may be well enough, and even find a faint hint of support in Deuteronomy. The authority that each historical civilizational law had for those who lived under it has *something* in common with the others, something universally human, the binding character of the vocation (however understood) to exist as a civilized society, and not merely as a natural society. That historical vocation is the foundation of various histories. All history, if there is to be any history at all, will be the history of *some* law, the history of what has become of that immanent demand to be governed by law and not by natural impulse. Yet we have to be careful not to jump to the conclusion that what Israel, China, and Rome received was essentially one and the same: not only are their laws different, and their conceptions of law different, but their relation to the work of God in history is different. If the many historical vocations are at root one, and if the idea of a "vocation" is not to be drained of all meaning, they must constitute different reflections of the one paradigmatic vocation, the one on which the Deuteronomists fix our attention uniquely, the self-demonstration of God as Israel's redeemer and lawgiver.

We return, however, to the point from which we began: the authority of law cannot subsist in the present tense alone. Law that rules settled existence in a home on the earth must look

back to the terms that have been set for civilized existence, to the
context in which it arose in the natural human and nonhuman
world, for only so can it restrain the destructive opposition of
human action and natural constraints, correcting the narrow
species-self-interest that imagines the human race as master of
the material and spiritual world. "Are the trees in the field men
that they should be besieged by you?" is part of an ancient law
of siege preserved in Deuteronomy (20:19). At the same time,
it must look *forward* to the achievement of a fuller harmony of
world and society, a stage of civilization yet to be reached, and
it cannot be understood apart from a horizon of fulfillment to
which it points us. If we abstract law from historical fulfillment,
we make of it a pure ideal of performance, unworldly, inhuman,
and ungodly. The immediate tensions and antinomies of human
life in the world are directed toward what has yet to be achieved.
As the *normative* form, law is also the *eschatological* form of
God's gift to humankind. It accounts, we may say, for the reality
of moral history, allowing us to take stock of what has effectively
been achieved as well as of what still remains unfulfilled.

THE LAWFUL USE OF LAW

Which means that law, while explicitly the bearer of *command*,
is implicitly the bearer of *promise*. And this dual character of
law, its outer and its inner reality, is the reason why Israel was
constantly involved in critique of its own law-governed practices. We often think of the critique of law as a special contribution of Christianity, but it was a Jewish contribution first. There
was a wisdom that could say, "Be not righteous overmuch!"
(Eccl. 7:16). But Deuteronomy itself, with its impassioned objections to the conflicting and confused shape of law in its own
day, affords a key example of how law generates the critique of
law. Behind all laws is the demand of law itself:* the *presenting*

---

* For further comments, see my *Ways of Judgement*, Bampton Lectures
(Grand Rapids: Eerdmans, 2005), 186–90.

law conceals but also discloses the *vocation* to law. That dynamic of self-concealment and self-disclosure is the authentic sign of law as a living historical reality, not merely a dead constraint. When the Pauline author of the Pastoral Epistles declares gnomically, "The law is good, if any one uses it lawfully," he meant to echo the warning against legal categories deployed abstractly, outside the context of moral promise and fulfillment. Legal formulae, he goes on, have a bias to negative categories: "the law is not laid down for the just but for the lawless and disobedient, for the ungodly and sinners, for the unholy and profane" (1 Tim. 1:8–9). Law lacks the conceptual resources to explore the many paths of moral self-fulfillment, for which it requires to be filled out by a language of the good.

How, then, can we describe the "lawful" use of law? First of all, it formulates *demands* implicit in the goods and evils we recognize. It allows the good to govern practical reason through prescription and prohibition. Laws are not, like goods, real elements of created being, but formulations of practical reason, both prescriptive and prohibitive, which come to bear upon us in history, directing us in the states of affairs in which we must act. The good itself, complex and manifold as creation itself, is broken down by law to become practically intelligible as general types of demand addressed to typical situations of decision: "You shall not kill," "you shall not commit adultery," "you shall not steal," etc. And since law is self-correcting, it can evolve more complex distinctions and qualifications of these general types, allowing practical reason to develop together with experience. All mature bodies of law have their "casuistry," their interpretation of principles in the light of complex realities. Yet even though it may become complex, law still simplifies by digesting an infinity of experience into defined formulae. It never reaches beyond the moral experience of the *past*. It travels behindhand of experience, following a reality that has unfolded, attempting to digest it retrospectively into typical directive principles, so that even its most complex formulations may still prove too rough and ready for new occasions. While implying a promise, it cannot actually predict. Though indefinitely open to further application and specification and able to speculate formally on contingencies—if such and such were to happen, the law *would require* such and such—law does not articulate a *demand* for every future situation, simply because every possible future situation has not yet been described in generic categories. No one concrete formula, then, can be "the" law, all by itself, as a wholly known quantity. Moreover, there is a limit to the complexity at which directive principles are useful; the point can be reached where law has become too complex for the ordinary uses of society. *Summum ius summa iniuria* was a sad truth recognized in republican Rome. When we refer to practical reason as "uncodifiable," what we mean is that interpretation and resolution of new challenges in the practice of judgment are an ongoing moral task, never completed in history. Law opens the way for judgment; it points to a receding horizon, beyond the scope of its formulations, and offers a categorical structure to give rational guidance to the judgment of new challenges as they arise. That truth is captured, rather inadequately, by the traditional concept of works of "supererogation"—that is, "beyond" the law. They lie beyond the *formula* of the law, but the law, pointing us beyond its own formulae, summons us to judge whether or not they are required of us.

The second contribution of law is to present the moral *demand* as *command*. A demand is something we recognize for ourselves, but a command implies social communication. The law has both internal and external uses; it is a constraint that each agent may freely impose on himself or herself, but also a constraint one agent may impose upon another. When we understand an action as required because commanded, we understand ourselves not simply as agents but as co-agents. We acknowledge the authority of a community over our action, an authority to which we hold others answerable and expect to be held answerable in our turn. Command envisages that agents will be implicated in each other's practical reasoning, that there will be a field of mutual authorization, formal or informal, in which what each person does is a matter of common responsibility. "Command" represents the directly social aspect of duty. One function of law is to map the social relations that generate authoritative commands, to construct them as a unitary public tradition, avoiding the chaos of authorities in competition. A developed law reflects the complexity of a social world. From the multilayered understanding of law that prevailed throughout the high Middle Ages—divine law, natural law, Mosaic law, evangelical law, the law of nations, positive ecclesiastical law and civil law, laws of sovereign jurisdictions including statutes, decrees, customs, privileges, dispensations, etc.—we can read off the medieval social universe, the unitary and civilized society of human beings complexly woven out of many strands of authoritative structure and relation, from the all-embracing command of God at one end to the precise authority to determine exceptional contingencies at the other. This construction had a far more profound effect on the medieval mind than what the scholars learned from Aristotle. It imposed restraints—on the powers of popes, kings, nobles, emperors, and clerics—but in doing so, recognized their functions as having precisely this and not that authority, each with its place in the firmament. Respectful of the fact that none of us can be born, live, and die in one social environment alone, but flourish only in response to many different social claims made upon us, it imposed an order on those claims. Law was an authority to rule authorities.

Social realities are not the *creation* of law, for our nature is social all the way down. But they are reborn, as it were, by being taken into the framework of law as "institutions." The authority conferred on a command by its social provenance is recognized and contained by law in a public institutional framework. My dead father's solemn wishes *ipso facto* command my respect. But they are reinforced, and at the same time controlled, by testamentary law. A court can rule how far my respect for them should run. This institutional framework for our natural lives we refer to as a "public tradition," an expression in which both words are load bearing. In speaking of it as "public," we distinguish it from our immediate awareness of the demand of God. The heart, the core of moral personality, is subject to divine scrutiny in ways that escape public scrutiny. We also distinguish it from natural social forms—family, shared interests, neighborhood, friendship, and so on—for it creates a social space to be shared with those *not* bound to us by such natural forms. In public we are strangers to one another, subject to one another's judgment "without respect of persons." In speaking of the public sphere as a "tradition," on the other hand, we recognize in it a continuity that both precedes and outlives all its participants. By participating in it we share the responsibilities and privileges of an antecedent and persisting identity unlike all natural and spontaneous identities. Brought to its present shape by constantly repeated judgments, this identity defines itself by a normative history, a prevailing political narrative that interprets the past selectively to give prominence to what will secure the public institutions as seems expedient for the time being. Each one of us participates in this identity, yet each one of us can transcend it in thought, can admire it and criticize it in due measure, can correct the biases of its narrative, and so on. This is not a spontaneous and immediate identity, like that conferred by the social forms we are born into; it is a creation of law, and therefore both a demand and a vocation.

To enable us to see more clearly the contribution law makes to moral thinking, there is a useful reflecting mirror: antinomianism. Originally this term, as deployed in the era of the Reformation, identified something we may describe as "public antinomianism," which is to say, a rejection of the process we have just described, the role of law in shaping the tradition of public identity. Our question, however, requires us to think also of a "conceptual antinomianism," which denies the correspondence between internal and immediate moral awareness and public normative principles. Law is the external, ethics the internal normative principle. Law has no place in ethics, since it is external to the agent who seeks to live in the light of the good. Behind this radical alternative there lies an assumption that the external-internal distinction corresponds to the distinction between *prescription* and *description*. Prescription is seen as the mode of public or external communication; immediate moral judgments are seen as essentially descriptive.

A recent philosophical fashion along these lines declares that it rejects "morality"—signalized by quotation marks and sometimes by an initial capital. First Bernard Williams and more lately Alasdair MacIntyre have popularized this way of identifying a Kantian style of autonomous universal prescriptivism. "Morality" is characterized by MacIntyre (1) as being essentially prescriptive; (2) as claiming universal validity for its prescriptions; and (3) as having no foundations in reality, religious or otherwise, and so being autonomous.* His objection to it is that it persistently confronts those who follow it with an insoluble dilemma, in which the question is not, as it should be, which of a number of possible paths they should follow, but whether to stick with "Morality" or abandon all moral concerns whatever. Williams wished to replace "Morality" with an ultimate truth about the individual agent's own interior commitments; the reason for moral dilemmas was that the agent did not know what he or she was ultimately committed to. That is something Williams thought we can and should know about ourselves, not merely something we should "decide," but in practice we often do not know it. We may interpret this as an atheist revision of Augustinian anthropology, the good understood as the core of a self with which we have dangerously lost touch. Williams's objections, then, are directed against the universality and prescriptivism of "Morality," not against its autonomy. MacIntyre, challenging Williams's individualism, wishes to replace "Morality" not with an Augustinian truth about the self but with

* Alasdair MacIntyre, *Ethics in the Conflicts of Modernity: An Essay on Desire, Practical Reasoning, and Narrative* (Cambridge: Cambridge University Press, 2016), 65: Morality is "a set of rules, ideals and judgments concerning duties and obligations distinguished from religious, legal, political and aesthetic rules, ideals and judgments."

an Aristotelian truth about human flourishing in community. He objects to its claim to autonomy, not its claim to universal validity. From which it is clear that MacIntyre, objecting to autonomy and supporting universal validity, has less in common with Williams, who objects to universal validity and champions autonomy, than he would like us to believe. Of the three elements supposed to be objectionably combined in "Morality," the only one they agree in rejecting is prescription, the form of a moral truth mediated as law. They refuse to accept law as a *valid social mediation* of our moral knowledge.

For MacIntyre, celebrated for advising moral philosophers to pay attention to traditional social practices and beliefs, this is an uncomfortable position to end up in.* It appears that the tradition he champions must be a tradition of natural community alone, something we drink in with our mother's milk or learn from our earliest instructors, not something for which we depend on the practical traditions of organized society. But a tradition of that kind would lack a social vocation, which is to say, a promise directed to the form of history. Unenviably for someone who has understood what is wrong with ahistoricism, he conceives that each agent who has not been corrupted by philosophers into believing universal prescriptivism takes up the question of human flourishing with a clean slate, with no inher-

---

* I leave to others the decision on how consistent *Ethics in the Conflicts of Modernity* is with MacIntyre's more celebrated earlier writings. But there are clearly some familiar features. His "human flourishing," a more complicated cousin of animal flourishing, is frankly naturalistic and leaves no room to see morality as a developing historical culture, with its roots in law and its fulfillment in the Spirit. Supplying "Morality" with a historical *Sitz im Leben* in early modern mercantilism, he denies the role of tradition in early modern civilization, and especially the role of religious tradition, which intellectual historians have been inclined to emphasize. He ignores whatever of antiquity is not Aristotle, especially the development of law in the Mediterranean basin and its elaboration by the rabbis and Jesus of Nazareth. He ignores the vast predominance of law-based morality in the Western Middle Ages, not least in Thomas Aquinas, whom he continues to invoke selectively as the best exponent of Aristotle and (implausibly) the source of his own ideas.

itance of public rules, no thought that what is binding for others is binding for himself or herself and vice versa. Essentially, with no "history of salvation," as the theologians would express it.

THE CRITIQUE OF LAW AND THE FORM OF HISTORY

Law as a *mediation* for the perception of the good (of social flourishing, of the personal vocation, or whatever) is essentially a *historical* reality in which the good appears. History, if we are to talk about such a thing at all, is precisely not open to immediate discernment. It is a coherence of the whole of time, the forgotten as well as the remembered, the unanticipated as well as the often recounted. And since history is far too diverse in the types of its events and the vast scope of its transformations to imagine a coherence in terms of one type of event, that coherence can only, in the end, be a moral coherence, the unfolding of a consistent purpose toward a definite end. There are moments at which history may appear in that light immediately. The growth of civilization, the overcoming of distances between communities, the increasing abhorrence of violence—any of these may supply us with sufficient indications that history is moving in a moral direction to a moral end. But there are rather more moments in which we can see only confusing signals, or in which our hope is dashed. The sight and understanding we are given of history are provisional, given *in* seeking and *for* seeking. Faith in history imposes the labor of searching for positive clues and interpreting them well. And that is the point of the service rendered to moral thought by law: it supplies a tradition of normativity still open to the future, an anchor for the promise of future disclosure to hold firmly to.

It must have been more than frustrating for ancient Israel's prophets, those interpreters of current events who, like journalists today, carried considerable authority in their nation's life, when the Deuteronomic legislators declared that prophetic authority could be recognized only after the fact, when what was predicted had come to pass (Deut. 18:22). We might suspect the Deuteronomists of trying to shut down prophetic insight altogether. But there is a better reading of their intentions: they were defending a logic inherent in all interpretation of history, namely, that it cannot be validated in a single moment. They wanted to curb the *immediacy* of an authority that acknowledged no disciplines of reflection. It was not the journalists they wanted to shut down (to continue the simile) but the headlines. Prophetic insight, given at a particular juncture of affairs, needed other moments of time and other junctures of affairs to prove itself. The status of the prophetic message, therefore, must be something like a hypothesis, open to justification and validation from further observations. And, since the work of God in history, though often surprising, was essentially coherent, the form its validation must take would be that of coherence with the law.

And so it is said that "one jot and tittle" of the law shall not pass away till all is fulfilled (Matt. 5:18 RV). The promise of the law is valid in all its detailed complexities. An evangelical proclamation about history cannot simply sweep law aside. The jot and the tittle, understood correctly, were not mere details of *prescription*, unsupported niceties of conduct required for no obvious reason, but details of *moral description* won from experience of the complex world of action. They are the fine brushwork of the historically unfolding world to which our action must respond, the world that is the object and site of God's work. To lose interest in the complexities of law is to lose interest in the providential work of God and to connive at bad descriptions. This is the antinomian temptation of the evangelical consciousness: what we take to be a message of good news for the world ceases to be addressed to the realities we actually live among and becomes, instead, an empty boast of another world. But if we have understood the central point, that to use law lawfully we must use it historically, bringing it to bear on the times we live in, we are protected not only against antinomian immediacy but against the misuse of law that antinomianism always suspects, the nomistic immediacy that treats law, by virtue of its power to create institutions, as itself the source of lived human reality. Legal institutions may indeed become surrogates for the original gift of God; the institutionalized world can replace the real world in our imaginations, the truths mediated by tradition can substitute for the truth of God's purposes, so that we lose sight of goods that transcend social institutions, supremely the goods of love and truth. We are no better off with such a de-historicized law, which does away with all past moral and social experience and all anticipatory hope and promise, and places us under the immediate direction of the public realm. These are real dangers, which the critique of law must warn us against. But rightly pursued, it will not reject the law but train us to look behind it to the historical fulfillment that lies concealed within it.

To the eyes of *institutional* law a multitude of practical possibilities for good and ill lie outside the established legal distinctions of commanded and forbidden, forming a kind of moral no-man's-land, a sphere of indifference. Yet they are full of possibilities for our good and ill, which from the moral point of view are far from indifferent. That message is forcibly expressed by the parable of the Good Samaritan in Saint Luke's version, which is presented as a conversation between Jesus and a lawyer. Having proposed in the wisest rabbinic fashion that the whole law is organized under the two commands of love for God and neighbor, the lawyer quite naturally asks about the definition of the terms involved: "Who is my neighbor?" The story that follows is designed to expose the inadequacy of that way of framing the question. The priest and Levite who ignore the need of the wounded man are likely to have asked that question, and to have found an answer: perhaps any duties they had to him would count as "imperfect," or perhaps "supererogatory." The Samaritan, who presumably has not asked that question, has discovered, unlooked for, a concrete opportunity to *realize* the good of neighborhood. There is an often-noticed disequilibrium between the reference of "neighbor" in the lawyer's question and in Jesus's answer. The neighbor in the law is the one *to whom* love is extended; the neighbor in the story is the one *who showed mercy*. This difference does not point to a more or less expansive account of the scope of neighbor love; it points to the law behind the law, a demand more primitive than any formulation that can be brought to bear in critique upon all formulations, a demand arising from God's gift, who puts it in our way that we can *be*, and therefore can have, neighbors.

In another famous saying, Jesus summed up the critique of law provocatively: "Judge not, that you be not judged" (Matt. 7:1). This may suggest to us, as it did to Max Scheler, that the whole moral depth of another person is inaccessible to judgment. But it also suggests that judgment out of turn not only misses the truth of the other person but misses the truth of judgment itself. It presumes a certain *kind* of truth as wholly normative, a truth of evidence, a truth of accepted rules of public procedure. To commit ourselves wholly to judgment is to give ourselves over to be known as public truths are known, which is superficially. It is not that the law can ever be detached from a foundation in truth; but if it begins from a truth of its own, a surface representation of public history allowing other truths to be lost sight of, it may induce a kind of selective blindness. Saint Paul's fascinating allegory on Moses's veil expresses perfectly the problematic character of public moral tradition. Law constructs a world that intervenes like a veil between our common life and the reality of God's purposes. Legal forms are mediating placeholders for something more dynamic, a radiance of divine appearance that lies behind the representations of the law. The task of the evangelist, he goes on, unlike that of the legislator, is to communicate "with unveiled face," exposed to the truth of the transforming glory made known in history (2 Cor. 3:18).

That image directs a glaring light on our contemporary disillusionment with the truths of the public world. Popular discourse is dissatisfied with what it calls the "politically correct," that set of doctrines that is forged to establish an appearance of common agreement more as a convenience to institutions than as a serious attempt to represent moral reality. Public judgment seems to distort and destroy attempts to envisage the true and the good. This coarsens the quality of moral discernment. Wisdom, as the ancient Jewish text tells us (Wis. 7:22–24), is subtle and refined, moving from one end of the universe to the other, but the demand for solidary conformity makes us stand in one place and repeat one truth like a slogan, over and over again. The common good, which ought to be rich and varied, is reduced to the logic of the single-issue campaign and the pathos of protest. Questions requiring complex negotiation are reduced to a formal opposition between a more adventurous and a more defensive stance, the ubiquitous "left and right" of democratic politics. Juridicalization takes over the very self-knowledge of the individual; for once I am prevailed upon to see myself as a bearer of rights, a living demand on others' recognition, I quickly forget how to see myself as an effective agent. The life-giving questions I need to ask about myself and the service for which I have been placed in the world are cut short by my enforced persona as a permanent plaintiff.

So there is a perennial and persistent need to think *behind* instituted laws and their institutions, to realities that hold to account not only institutional and legal demands but also internal uses of the law, demands self-imposed, and so on. One historical attempt to do this, exposing the idea of law to the measure of created goodness, was presented in the Christian world under the name of "natural law," a phrase that had a paradoxical sound even before the modern conception of nature made the paradox seem intolerable. For the essential point in speaking of a natural law was to incorporate the self-critique into the very concept of law, to recall that law's authority never sprang from the fact that it was posited but from the fact that it reveals reality. Within the medieval jurisprudence, natural law was a part of divine law—that part that was communicated universally in the act of creation and relied on no further revelation. The intention of its greatest early modern exponents, especially Vitoria in the sixteenth century and Grotius in the seventeenth, was not merely to restrain legal positivism and political absolutism, though that was important to them, but to describe a foundational moral rationality by which the subsequent development of law could be evaluated. Reception of Grotius in the English-speaking world, confined as it has been to broad-brush intellectual history and lacking in textual discipline, has largely failed to grasp that the account of natural law is used not primarily to secure *freedoms* but to ground an argument about history, the continuous development of civilization within Christendom, led by evangelical law, "law in its most perfected form, attached . . . to the promise of a supernatural state."* In that Christian jurisprudence, natural law had the first word in framing questions but not the last word in answering them.

It is tempting, with the foreshortened perspective allowed by intellectual history, to suppose that the collapse of natural law was simply the result of its inherent weaknesses. Yet the period of its unchallenged influence was long, many times longer, in fact, than the period of skepticism that followed it. It was one of those ideas that has to be called "successful," not merely because everyone shared it, but because its effects were so very positive for so very long. When the rival pretensions of institutions, civil and ecclesiastical, were negotiated in Europe, it exercised a constructive and restraining influence, keeping the creature's relation to the Creator always in view. It proved adaptable to different philosophical and theological styles, and was cherished by theologians on both sides of the Reformation divisions. When natural law fell from influence in later modernity, it was because the new concept of nature no longer supported the paradox of a nature that was at the same time a law, though here, too, what we said about the concept of nature in the last lecture still holds good: an idea that no longer has the

---

* Hugo Grotius, "The Right of War and Peace (2.20.10)," in *From Irenaeus to Grotius: A Sourcebook in Christian Political Thought*, ed. Oliver O'Donovan and Joan Lockwood O'Donovan (Grand Rapids: Eerdmans, 1999), 811.

status of a commonplace in changed civilizational conditions does not necessarily lose its illuminative power or its usefulness as a critical tool. With the eighteenth-century shift to empiricism what had been understood as foundational moral reality came to look like no more than consensus. And that robbed natural law of its normative force, since authority resting on consensus cannot bind the dissenter. But its collapse created a vacuum since filled by the distinctively modern conception of natural rights,* essentially plural, founded on a multitude of singular identities without a cosmic and social coherence, and therefore at war with law as the promise and demand of coherence.

Even had the concept of natural law remained unchallenged in Western civilization, we should need to be aware of its limitations. In patristic theology it had mediated effectively between the realities of creation and the demands of morality, a reminder of what is always supposed by the idea of a moral law. But this meant that from the beginning there was too little emphasis on the connection of law and promise. And with the consequent lack of an eschatological hope, creation, too, proved to be an unstable idea, so that medieval and early modern theology lost sight of both in pursuit of their concerns with the divine government of the world. Building the radiance of the Creator's glory into law reinforced the impression that the whole content of divine revelation was prescriptive, and with this the true relationship of divine and human action was turned on its head. The ease with which creation could be subsumed into nature and nature into law made it possible for this to happen. As we often see in our contemporary environmental

---

* For further discussion, see Joan Lockwood O'Donovan, "The Challenge and the Promise of Proto-Modern Political Thought," in *Bonds of Imperfection: Christian Politics Past and Present* (Grand Rapids: Eerdmans, 2004), 137–66; and Joan Lockwood O'Donovan, "Rights, Law and Political Community," *Transformation* 20, no. 1 (2003): 30–38.

discussions, "creation" can quickly become a mere cipher for stable natural recurrences. The complaint about the absence of promise was expressed most forcibly, perhaps, in Luther's famous intellectual strategy of *Unterscheidung*, "distinction," where law and gospel were treated as dialectical opposites running throughout history, a "strange work" of divine providence accompanying a "proper work" of divine grace. Law belonged to history, and in a certain sense directed it, but always provisionally, so as to be superseded and overcome. For Luther the fulfillment of history must be *freedom*, by which he meant the perfect reconciliation of the inner self with ordered social life in mutual love. Such freedom as law could give us, he thought, was merely forced. So the idea of history is constructed on a tension of past and future, the closed past opening out into the indeterminate future in which the secrets of God's purpose lie. The law, having shaped the idea of history, must be understood as ended, a preliminary movement in the activity of God's grace and not the whole of it.

History is an easier idea to bite on than to swallow. We have spoken of history as "having" a form; it would be more precise to say that it "is" a form, a unique form imposed on the successive events of time. To understand "time" as "history" is to refuse the superficial appearance of time as formless and inconsequential. As that which we know by narrative, history involves a before-and-after, an "earlier and latter," a "first this, then that." It involves a *direction of fulfillment*, in which the former good becomes a later good, and a later good "satisfies" the former good. Thinking these two thoughts together means thinking a moral coherence of earlier and later time, a continuity of event that allows and requires narration. Narrative is the form of discourse that corresponds to history as the form of time. History is an idea very easy to collapse onto one side or the other, either investing the idea of the good in a detached moment without continuity, so that "history" is mere "historicity," *this* moment as opposed to *that*, or conforming the idea of fulfillment to that of natural regularity, so that the new is simply "what was bound to happen."* There is the view that the past is remote from us in its pastness, another and different time; there is, alternatively, the view that the past is always present to us, determining us through the inevitability of its causality. Both these collapsed forms of the idea of history have been criticized under the label "historicism," though they collapse the idea of history in opposite directions. What they have in common is the determination to take time, rather than being, as the ultimate determinant of knowledge. On such a basis, of course, narrative is excluded from knowledge, even from the knowledge of time, for narrative is sustained between *two* poles: the *subject* of the narrative and *what becomes* of the subject. It is all the more necessary, then, to insist on the theological point that history as the form of time is necessarily the redemption of time. Time is not redeemed by novelty, or even by continuity. It requires a "direction" and a corresponding "fulfillment," involving that which is *not* reducible to time.

Jesus's proclamation of the kingdom of God could be summed up in two propositions: (1) there is no form of history that is not an *ultimate* form; (2) there is no form of history that is not a *moral* form, a disclosure of the good. From these two propositions the modern concept of "history" derives— speaking always, of course, of the philosophical concept of history, not of how historians understand their practice. The word "history," as it first came to use in ancient Greece, meant simply an "inquiry" or "investigation"; attached to the kind of narrative we describe as "a history," it was always used in the plural. The historians' histories are still essentially plural, even if the discipline is referred to in the singular. Each and every "history" offers a rational account of some discrete series of events. Such "histories" have formal features in common, since the investigation of the past imposes certain common formal

* This was the sense in which George Grant dismissed "time as history" as "not a conception we are fitted for"; *Time as History*, Toronto Canadian Broadcasting Corporation, 1969, 45.

disciplines; what they do not have is a single object in common, a rational account of the sequence of all events whatever. When Greek-speaking theologians first framed the idea of a unified history, they did not use that noun but spoke of "the *oikonomia*," the "administration" of world time by the direction of God. And it is as well to be clear that the step from many "histories" to one "history," or *oikonomia*, involves an act of faith and would have no justification if the *moral* project of human life did not demand that the unitary idea should be thought. "The darkness is passing away and the light is beginning to shine" (1 John 2:8, author's translation). In that declaration we meet the core experience from which the concept of history is generated. If that experience is valid, the emergence of agency and action becomes the central and universal theme of history. And "history" is then *ipso verbo* the history of civilization and of developing wisdom.

Which presents a paradox. Action is limited and determinate, purposed at a certain point in time in circumstances that are, by the very nature of time, temporary. Acts are effective only if they are wholly accommodated to their moment in time, formed of definite purposes envisaging definite ends. That is why there are many "histories" narrating many actions at different moments in time. Yet if we place ourselves in the position of actors, we find we cannot act without looking for something more than a particular moment. Each and every act we lay our hand to is viewed before a receding horizon of future time that is in principle indefinite, which we know must either confirm or annihilate the effectiveness of what we undertake. We may think we see far enough into the future to know that time can only annihilate it, in which case we shall make a feint of graceful philosophical withdrawal from the active life, with a Puck-like observation on its futility—"Lord, what fools these mortals be!" But that gesture can never be final. The next time we wonder what we should do, we shall search the horizon again for a sign of confirmation and seek to make our action effective. The idea of something *ultimately or decisively effective* is an idea that cannot be eliminated from the value we set on purposeful action.

Take the example of a small act of kindness that may lighten the horror of a group of people whose life is doomed—on their way to a firing squad, perhaps, or in an aircraft falling from the sky into the ocean. The poignancy of such a gesture arises from the contrast between its immediate ineffectiveness and the persistent moral faith that such acts will ultimately be vindicated. The effect of a small kindness in such a setting is that of a *credo*: the disaster unfolding here and now cannot be the last or decisive thing; a horror such as this will in the end be overcome. To take a more modest and less horrific example: it is surely incredible that anyone would ever undertake the long labor of writing a serious book without believing that whatever attention the book may command or fail to command from publishers, readers, and reviewers, the writing of it somehow contributes to an outcome that will justify what may look like a waste of life. It is an intuitive connection of ideas that to every effective act there corresponds an effective agent, and to the effective agent there is due an ultimate vindication in the course of time. We are agents essentially, not accidentally, and stand before a temporal horizon that must ultimately confirm or bring to nothing what we do and what we are. Together with what we are there stands or falls, so far as we can perceive it, the history of the world. History is the conception of a form of time in which the vindication of our agency finds a place. A life that comes to nothing is a chronicle of wasted time, and "waste" is precisely what constitutes time as ahistorical. History is a conception of time as directed to the justification of our living and acting.

THE FORM OF HISTORY AND CHRISTOLOGY

So we open the door to a faith in the moral fulfillment of history, or the historical fulfillment of morality. A natural theology, if it takes that faith seriously, can conceive of the occurrence of a decisive moment when the moral form of history becomes clear, a moment of disclosure that both fulfills and promises fulfillment. A moral philosophy can, and perhaps must, reach the view articulated by Scheler, that "the person" is conceivable only concretely, as a particular historical person bound into a particular historical community of persons. This train of thought brings natural theology and moral philosophy as close to a Christology as could be imagined within the limits of abstract thought. But they cannot form a Christology. They can speak of what may or must in principle be the case somewhere and somehow, if the supposition of a faith in history is valid. They can formulate the *idea* of a decisive moment of moral history and of a particular person appearing uniquely within it. But to speak of a Christ is to do more than form the idea of a kind that can have only one instance; it is to identify the one instance. Christology requires an ostensive demonstration, a "Look here!" that lies beyond the repertoire of the moral philosopher or natural theologian. It requires a narrative theology to fill the empty form with substance.

Hans Urs von Balthasar proposed that we describe Christ as "the concrete categorical imperative."* Enlisting that Kantian motif in the service of Christology, he was able to describe the christological moment of history as a moral moment. He could affirm the Kantian conviction that the sphere of the good in action is coherent, and whatever is done well corresponds to a universal form, while maintaining against Kant that the conceptual key to the good in action was a once-and-for-all historical reality, a *concrete personal* form. If there is such a thing as a categorical imperative, a normative form governing human action in all types and circumstances, it is not a principle but an acting

* Hans Urs von Balthasar, "Nine Propositions on Christian Ethics," in H. U. von Balthasar, J. Ratzinger, and H. Schürman, *Principles of Christian Morality*, trans. Graham Harrison (San Francisco: Ignatius, 1986), 79.

person who appeared at a certain point in history and can be told of narratively. Kant supposed Christ's life to be the supreme example of the formal norm; Balthasar, in response, found the moral authority of the form in the fact that it was historically accomplished, changing forever the terms on which human agents live. "Christ," Saint Paul once said, "is the end of the law" (Rom. 10:4). Without that historical horizon morality collapses back into regular patterns, and philosophical talk of "history," evacuated of narrative content, withers into mere "historicality," a pseudo-concept that seems to mean little more than a blind sense of the here and now without connection to a definite there and then. It is "historicality" in the absence of "history" that makes law destructive, locks us into the grip of the powers prevailing in the particular age in which we find ourselves.

The point was made concisely by Saint Paul again: "The letter kills; it is the spirit that gives life" (2 Cor. 3:6 RV). Law has a spirit that must animate it, and that spirit is a spirit of historical form and anticipation. Deprived of anticipation, the law cannot be lived with, for we live by looking forward, however short our view may be in that direction. From that forward view we are not entitled to leap boldly into speaking of a positive hope. Anticipation is not hope; or rather, it is not *yet* hope. Hope depends on the conscious excess of practice over knowledge, on a particular anticipation that reaches out beyond its cognitive indications. We could, with difficulty, banish hope from our list of virtues and somehow continue living; it would be a life of caution and stern resignation, governed by the resolve never to form anticipations that could be disappointed. But without anticipation we cannot live, except perhaps in a marginal way in such pathological states as deep depression. The cognitive gaze on the future, though revealing very little, cannot be redirected, for without it we cannot be active. Either we shall read the law as supporting anticipation, with a promise of fulfillment on which hope can gain a purchase, or we shall find it an executioner to cut us off from the land of the living. That is the element of truth

underlying the exaggerated antinomian rejection of "morality."
It is exaggerated, because the law *may* be read prophetically, or,
as ancient Christian writers frequently expressed it, "spiritually."
In our final lecture, therefore, we consider the role of the Spirit
in Ethics, the gift of a fulfillment in moral history, which makes
divine action effective in human life and action.

SIX

Spirit and the Justification of Agency

The end of history, according to the proclamations of the historical religions, is a *moral* fulfillment, the confirmation and completion of human agency in an effective accomplishment of good. This general picture can be elaborated in a number of ways. There is an idealist proposition that the goal of history is *freedom*; there is a nomistic proposition that the goal of history is *conformity*; there is a quietist proposition that the goal of history is *enjoyment*. When we come to understand how these apparently contrasting definitions in fact complement one another, we begin to see what is meant by effective accomplishment. It is the freedom to live in conformity with a world order that invites enjoyment rather than struggle. To bring these aspects of agency together and deepen them, I shall lay claim to a theological term and describe the ultimate goal of history as *justification*. "Justification" means, and can only mean, justification *of agency*, both divine and human. To see history as justification is to see it as vindicating a world in which divine and human action are decisive against the imputation or suspicion of failure and incoherence.

The failure of agency we speak of in traditional terms as "sin," which names both a subjective failure of will and an objective defeat of performance. It is the broadest term for the frustration of enacted good. The disappearance of the agent from among the themes of Ethics, of which Scheler complained, corresponds precisely to a disappearance of agency from commonplace

moral thinking, a reduction of thought about practical good
and evil to questions of what *ought to be* done—done by "someone," that is, or by some wholly unspecified "we"—avoiding the
question of *who* is given to do *what*. The disappearance of the
agent is an inhibition of moral imagination, an incapacity to
think through what it means to be the agents we thoughtlessly
assume we are. The "justification" of human agency is God's effective affirmation that what we assume we are, we shall indeed,
by *his* doing, come to be, agents who are effective in doing some
good. The justification of divine agency is the demonstration
that creation has given us a world that is hospitable to effective
action. That is the divine determination of history that brings
us back to the point from which we began the last lecture, that
a morally directed history is conceivable only as a divine initiative of self-disclosure. God's purposes can and will confirm and
elicit agency, making the history of the world, that history of
many histories, one effective realization of the good, justifying
the many lesser actions, good or evil, effective or ineffective as
they may be on their own terms, that have gone to make it up.
Dietrich Bonhoeffer called it "the profound mystery of history
as such" that "free action, as it determines history, recognises
itself ultimately as being God's action."*

COOPERATION

But how can we imagine such a coinvolvement of divine and human agency? Some expositions of the doctrine of "grace" have
seemed to leave this question unanswered and to generate the
destructive alternative: either God acts, or the creature acts, the
two agencies competing, as it were, for the same limited space
of free self-disposal. And since God is infinite and the creature
finite, such a competition is bound to end badly, either with
the exposure of creaturely freedom as chimerical or with the

* Dietrich Bonhoeffer, *Ethics*, Dietrich Bonhoeffer Works 6 (Minneapolis: Fortress, 2005), 151.

self-removal of God to leave room for creaturely freedom. God's self-removal need not be conceived as his *total* absence from the work of providence. It may simply be conceived as a partition of roles, such as was proposed, disastrously, by Theodore of Mopsuestia: "It is up to God's grace to call us, to bestow his Spirit upon us, and to set future promises before us; but to remain firm in the faith is our job, not his."* But if, as the Western church tended to think, it would be a very insufficient grace that was withdrawn at the decisive moment merely to heap upon us the reproach of having failed under our own steam, it may alternatively be conceived as a partition of ontological planes, a distinction of finite and infinite, resolutely separating talk of divine action from talk of human action so that the two are never part of a shared narrative of interaction.

Whatever possibilities this ontological partition may create for interpreting *experience*—at one level I recognize a purely human experience, at another the experience of a divine presence—as applied to *action* it is incoherent. Action is by definition determinate, which is to say, finite. There is no action that is not this or that action, beginning at one point and ending at another. There is no action that does not communicate with, intervene upon, and affect the conditions of, enabling, supporting, or frustrating other actions that have preceded it or are synchronous with it. To speak of divine action it is not enough to posit an infinite being that authorizes and presides over history as a whole; one must suppose an infinite being that can engage in finite ways within a finite world. "Infinite agency" would be absolute, effective on all events and actions without distinction, allowing no difference in event between the sanctified, the common, and the ungodly. "Infinite action" would not be action at all. God's infinity is manifest *through* action, not *as* action. A first or last act could be infinite, an act of creation or of de-creation. But within the history of the world, as Barth says,

---

* Theodore of Mopsuestia, Fragment from *Commentary on Galatians*, Patrologia Graeca 66:909.

God gives himself "time, space and opportunity" to act. "We have to speak of an *analogia operationis*," he goes on, God active in the same time and the same temporal conditions as human agents, performing some deeds and not other deeds, resisting some purposes and supporting others "on the basis of his own good-pleasure."* He does not indifferently bring all things to pass but acts to command some actions and allow others, shaping the universe of actual and possible human actions to bring about one final purpose within which human activity belongs, the goal of history or the will of God.

Only mechanical force obeys the law that the greater always swallows the lesser. The current of the river absorbs the energy of the tributary streams; the wall absorbs the momentum of the vehicle that crashes into it. It is a mechanical model of agency that creates the false dilemmas of the theory of grace. Agents, even those with very different powers, do not swallow each other up in that way. A demonstration of this lies in that most familiar of human experiences, cooperation, in which two or more wholly free agents act together to achieve one purpose without loss of integrity to either. Not only is cooperation familiar to us; it is the *primary* experience we have of action. From the baby who learns to walk supported under the arms by parents to the dying patient sipping water from a cup held to the lips by a nurse, our experience of action is that of doing things *with* people. The solitary agent—the poet alone among the crags and streams composing verse—is the exception, and even that exception, as Wordsworth is the first to point out, is only apparent. All civilized activity is founded on the principle that acting together enhances the effectiveness of participating agents. St. Andrews University presents Gifford Lectures, and so does O'Donovan; yet the occasion is the same and there is only one set of lectures. There is nothing here that should puzzle

* Karl Barth, *Church Dogmatics* III/3 (Edinburgh: T&T Clark, 1960), §48.3, p. 47; Ger. p. 55; §49.2, p. 102; Ger. p. 116.

us. We need not locate the university and the lecturer on different ontological planes; it is simple cooperation.

It is a common misunderstanding that cooperation implies equality between the partners, and this leads to unfounded suspicion of many cooperative endeavors that incorporate a degree of inequality.

Cooperation implies, to be sure, that the partners have an *equal freedom to act*; they are, in fact, necessarily equal, since freedom of agency is an absolute, not a graduated property. But cooperation does not imply that the partners bring an *equal power* to their endeavor, or that their functions are equally important to it. If I possess just one share in a corporation, the larger shareholders will have greater power at a general meeting than I do; but my freedom is precisely the same as theirs, a freedom to be present, to ask a question, to vote as I judge best, to withdraw my investment, and so on. Complex cooperation depends on differentiated roles and initiatives: the university has authority over who shall lecture on the Gifford foundation, the lecturer has authority over what shall be said in those lectures; each authority is final on its own terms. But authority in cooperative relations may also have degrees: students have less authority than their teachers over what needs to be taught and learned, though they have a decisive authority in the decision whether or not they will enroll in that university; patients have less authority than physicians over what treatments should be applied to their condition, though a decisive authority over whether they will submit to those treatments. And so on. Only one form of cooperation, in fact, is defined by total *absence* of authority, and that is pure friendship. Friendship is a treasure in itself and is built on cooperation; but it does not always get things done.

The quantitative misunderstanding that gives rise to an unjustified suspicion of unequal cooperation also gives rise to a suspicion of the whole idea of divine-human cooperation. That God is sovereign over history and the hearts of humankind may seem, necessarily, to abolish the freedom with which we worship and align our wills with his. But that is only seeming. The usefulness of the analogy of cooperation is that it offers us a paradigm for unequal but free cooperation that is enough to banish that a priori assumption. So let us speak—by analogy, to be sure, but an analogy that deserves some confidence—of a cooperative agency of God and man in shaping history. The Creator acts and the creature acts, though with unequal initiative; they are aligned in pursuit of purposes that are common to both, though with unequal clarity of conception.

THE SPIRIT

A theological name for this cooperative agency is ready and waiting: "the Spirit." "The Lord," said Saint Paul, "is the Spirit, and where the Spirit of the Lord is, there is liberty" (2 Cor. 3:18 RV)—by which, of course, he meant the liberty of perfectly ordinary human agents like himself to be "fellow workers" with God.

The reference of the term "Spirit" is famously fluid. It can be predicated of the Godhead as a whole, defining the divine milieu. It can identify the third person of the Godhead, whose property is to bear witness to the divine shaping of history and evoke participation in the work of the Father and the Son. Applied to human existence, it speaks of an openness to divine action that is not immanent in human nature but belongs to human fulfillment. To appeal to Barth once again: man "is" body and soul, but "has" the Spirit.* A purely natural anthropology would be dichotomous, physical and psychological, outer and inner; to speak of the "human spirit" is to point beyond nature to a historical fulfillment of the human calling. Whether referring especially to the breath that distinguishes living human beings from dead ones, or to the reflective capacity that allows

---

* Karl Barth, *Church Dogmatics* III/2 (Edinburgh: T&T Clark, 1960), §46.2, 354; Ger. 425.

them to transcend vital instincts and plot a path of free personal agency, or to the ecstasy that extends the intellectual gaze to the third heaven, in each case the language of spirit points to an excess, to *something else*, beyond what "naturally" meets the eye in the human appearance. There is always the suggestion of a dynamic horizon, an encounter with the transcendent. To call God Spirit and in the same breath to speak of the human spirit is to point to this encounter where divine agency "indwells" creaturely agency and human purposes become attuned to divine purposes. In John's Gospel the divine Spirit, while dwelling "in" us, never ceases to correspond to its mysterious name "Paraclete," which speaks of one *alongside* us, supporting and encouraging (John 14:16–17). Saint Paul speaks of an agreement of the divine Spirit with the human: "It is the Spirit himself bearing witness with our spirit that we are children of God" (Rom. 8:16). Even in quoting what looks like a dichotomous analysis of human impulses, "the desires of the flesh are against the Spirit, and the desires of the Spirit are against the flesh" (Gal. 5:17), he converts the appearance of a purely human division of powers into two opposed moral horizons,* a horizon of immanence and a horizon of transcendence. The opposition of the two prevents us, he says, from "doing whatever we will," for within the field of the Spirit's agency voluntary impulses are harnessed to serve an end of greater significance for the world. An ethics of the Spirit forges a unity at the very point where Ethics itself, as a reflective undertaking, is liable to split apart in two directions: into a realism that describes only the self-evident and superficial facts of human exertion, ignoring the historical and moral relations that make sense of them; and into an idealism that finds the good of humankind only in what has no being, an abstract horizon constituted by aspirations for the unachievable.

* For further discussion, see Oliver O'Donovan, "Flesh and Spirit," in *Galatians and Christian Theology: Justification, the Gospel, and Ethics in Paul's Letter*, ed. Mark W. Elliot et al. (Grand Rapids: Baker Academic, 2014), 271–84.

Yet in using the category of Spirit in Ethics some caution is needed. Invoking "the Spirit" too casually for explanatory purposes presents us with a familiar temptation: making God in the image of man. The spiritual is too easily conceived in terms of the inner structures of human nature. By speaking of "spirit" in emphasizing human powers that advance on animal characteristics, in emphasizing features that occur with more variable force in different individuals, or are especially complex and difficult to discern, we end up identifying "the Spirit" with communicative powers of language, with capacity for social co-operation or leadership, with intellectual comprehension and speculative thought, or with the socially unifying forces we may describe as the "spirit" of a common enterprise. In this way we come back to modeling Spirit upon nature—on the highest achievements of nature, to be sure, but on nature nonetheless. We project what we most admire about ourselves onto God as Spirit, and by that route end up with a fastidiously humanistic nature-divinity. That is why talk of the Spirit must begin from God's government of history, the inscrutable character of which exposes these self-projections to humiliation by events. It is in history that the Spirit is "given," to reveal God's purposes. In the New Testament, talk of the Spirit is centered upon the event of Pentecost, and the Gospels are not shy of speaking of a time, even in Jesus's lifetime, when "the Spirit had not been given" (John 7:39). At Pentecost the free initiative of divine agency commands us to be fulfilled in ways that we could never find the potential for within ourselves.

God's action in history works upon and with our creaturely nature not only in its most advanced and interesting forms, but even in its most elementary preconditions. And so the Spirit is called "the life-giver." If we ask what kind of life, we should answer, the life of historical agency *and therefore* the life of nature, too.

Sir James Macmillan, who recently composed a symphony on the Holy Spirit entitled *Le Grand Inconnu*, structured its three movements around images of elemental natural energy—wind, fire, and water. We may be tempted to dismiss these images of natural vitality as rather primitive metaphors. When we reflect on the immanent aspirations of human existence, we tend to think of the vital energies as no more than a material preparation for the higher goals of intellectual, moral, and social engagement. In divine action, however, the order is the other way round. Physical movement may be our earliest experience in life, but the giving-back of physical life will be God's *final* accomplishment in history. In nature the energies of wind, fire, and water come and go; it takes spirit, human and divine, to give them a teleological direction. Once drawn into the context of divine action, however, wind, fire, and water, too, become historical events and accomplishments effecting what the intellectual and moral realms could only imagine and wish for. The fulfillment of history, when it arrives, will realize, as nature cannot, the triumph of life over death, the healing of sickness, and the resurrection of the body. The apostolic witness to Jesus as the giver of the Spirit focuses on his miracles of healing and the resurrection of his body.

Events, to be sure, bear meanings that require interpretation. In another familiar pairing, "the spirit" is contrasted with "the letter." Letters inscribed on a page are "seen"; their meaning is not "seen" but "read." The divine voice within the motions of the soul and the community is never merely a primal vitality; it is an interpretation of vitality. So it was no less fitting that Sir James's work was a *choral* symphony, dominated by voices that speak or sing, the voice of God addressing creatures and the voice of creatures addressing God. If we must insist that the "meaning" of God's action is *life*, in its primary, vital sense, we must also insist that life itself is never other than a *meaningful communication*, which speaks as it lives. The Spirit who gives life gives freedom, and freedom implies the ability to discern meaning in events. We recognize, then, a new content for life itself. Life is not simply "the way of being of living things" but an address to us who live, a word that challenges us to insight and thoughtful response. The charismatic communities of the New Testament knew that the life of the Spirit demanded discernment, a communication of what did not lie on the surface of experience. What is presented theologically in the person of the Spirit is an ultimate unity of life and understanding, a vital effectiveness of purposeful agency that brings the original gift of living being to historical fulfillment. Through the Spirit the world's history appears in the form of good news, open to prophetic interpretation, centering upon the christological event, in which the goal of time has concrete expression. Jesus says in John's Gospel, the Spirit bears "witness to me" (John 15:26).

Once we have taken the measure of history, the innocence of a "natural" social morality, content with such fragmentary reasons as the practical context provides, is no longer open to us. It was never more than a preparation for the historical experience of life directed by God's purposes. In the accomplishment of those purposes we are summoned to believe. If we cannot believe in it, we are bound at least to imitate it with pseudohistorical realizations of morality in ersatz kingdoms of heaven conceived in materialist or political terms. That is the implication of living consciously in time: we will live in some recognizably apocalyptic expectation of disclosure, either conforming to the christological disclosure or aping it parodistically.* From either of these two points of view, belief and unbelief, "natural" ethics looks like a conscious reduction. In the sciences reduction is a legitimate heuristic technique to pursue specialized inquiries. If there are reductions in *moral* knowledge, they will be focused on special questions. Political concepts are reductions of this kind, postponing the ultimate questions about what is *good or evil to do* to more immediate questions about what *the common welfare requires to be done*, abstracting from the concrete whole of personal integrity to consult the demands of a regime

---

* On this point see Hans Urs von Balthasar, "Nine Propositions on Christian Ethics," in H. U. von Balthasar, J. Ratzinger, and H. Schürman, *Principles of Christian Morality*, trans. Graham Harrison (San Francisco: Ignatius, 1986), 100–104.

of law. Liberal rights, warrior hierarchies and landowner nobilities, work-based class solidarities, national loyalties—all these concepts serve a useful function in managing the societies constructed with their aid, but when taken for eternal moral truths, they become systematic illusions. In the eyes of the morally reflective they will always appear as artifices, concealing what we are and how we are placed. "When Adam delved and Evè span," the Lollard rhyme asked, "who was then the gentleman?" Or, we shall ask with equal justice, Who belonged to a social class? Who had a national identity? Who had natural rights?

Human Agency Conformed and Transformed

How, then, may we describe human agency in the light of the accomplishment of history? Let us begin by speaking of *faith*. Faith—it cannot be repeated too often—is a noun of action. It refers to an action of the mind, an internal action involving no bodily movement, yet an *active* action, not coming to rest in cognition of something, but in response to it. In believing someone or something we treat our perception as the ground for an active disposition, which will then lead out into various kinds of external action. Faith is the hinge by which the practical function of reason is freely suspended on the cognitive. It is a wholly commonplace action; we all perform it all the time, usually without thinking. In English it is conventional to speak of "belief" in relation to the more commonplace occurrences of this act, reserving "faith" for the more metaphysical and weighty, but this distinction, difficult to make in many languages, is secondary. "Faith" in the strong sense is simply a special case of what human agents do—special, because its object is special: the perception that history has been given a fulfillment and a purpose, that conscientious action is assured of its vindication. Such a perception, capable in itself and by its meaning of eliciting the active disposition, is grasped only as God's Spirit, in forming and shaping history, makes God's work known.

The act of faith in the strong sense, then, is a response to God's bringing history to a fulfillment. But it cannot depend on history without being part of history, itself open to fulfillment. Two verbs are used in the New Testament to speak of the fulfillment of the act of faith: "conform" and "transform." Both point to a new form that human agency assumes, not given in human nature but realized historically with the appearance of the Christ. The Spirit, in "conforming" the human agent to that new form, "transforms" the form that agency once had. It matters that we should be precise in how we describe this. The Christ form involves complete self-dedication, obedience to vocation, sacrifice. It is a form of love and mercy, and of courageously truthful communication. It is also, in the terms of its end, a form of death and resurrection, defeat and vindication. Any one of those descriptions, and others, may be decisively important at a particular juncture in determining a particular course of action. But each of these aspects is simply a "formed form"; no one of them is the "formative form," for that is the personal life of Christ himself. Which is why so many generalized conceptual descriptions of "Christlike" life sound hollow, sometimes sentimentally so and sometimes stridently, but in any case lacking the personal form of the Christ to give them substance. The discipline of conformity is a discipline of practical thought, requiring more than summary ideas to work with. What is given it is a gospel narrative, capable of being expounded in ideas, but always in many ideas, none of which expounds it conclusively and finally, except that one that has, as it were, been set aside precisely for the purpose of identifying the new form of life, which is "love." Love and the narrative of Christ interpret each other conclusively and comprehensively. Before venturing on any elaboration of the form of love, we have to encounter the narrative of the historical figure over and over again, always ready to find new angles, new challenges in it.

Besides these reductive summaries there is another mistake to avoid: the narrative is not *performable*, inviting reenactment, as though the earth could be peopled again by duplicate Mary

Magdalenes or Pontius Pilates, and we could all sign on as actors to play some well-known role. That would deny the form its power as a *promise* of new and fruitful realities. Life in the wake of the christological disclosure of history is still unscripted. The christological form allows new answers to new questions, answers in harmony with past questions and answers but never merely repetitious. The Spirit at Pentecost was experienced in a community that had the christological narrative at its center, but reached out to explore its power in new gifts of tongues and charisms, powers of articulate public speech and mutual service, all in the wake of the christological event, rejoicing in its accomplishment and exploiting the possibilities it had opened up.

The "form" of Christ is an expression that recurs constantly in the tantalizing drafts left by Dietrich Bonhoeffer for his never-completed *Ethics*, prominent especially in the early essay "Ethics as Formation," where the form of Christ is presented as the first reality of Christian Ethics, to which all other forms of moral deliberation are subordinate. It is the "cunning of serpents" to find good and evil not in *actions*, which may be wholly deceptive, but in *persons*, who in the crisis of his day, Bonhoeffer tells us, were morally larger than life, like saints and villains out of Shakespeare walking about in broad daylight—I presume he had Richard III and Macbeth in mind, not Beatrice and Benedict! In the burst of intellectual energy let loose by the coming of war Bonhoeffer seems to inhabit an apocalyptic moment, when "reality unveils itself," and instead of "grey on grey" (which was Hegel's description of philosophy), Ethics is constituted by the brilliant flash and impenetrable darkness of a thunderstorm. The form of Christ required the "simplicity of doves," sustaining an undivided gaze on God and "reality"—that is, what God is accomplishing in the world. Ethics must point to Christ and cry, "*Ecce homo!*" From that step the further step into freedom of action followed more or less immediately.

The philosophical and theological traditions of the Christian West, Bonhoeffer held, were at fault for introducing normative principles in between these two steps—the influence of Scheler, whom Bonhoeffer read, is clearly detectable here. These principles are the "rusty weapons" that modern-day Quixotes polish up in order to tilt at windmills, but they are "only tools in the hand of God, soon to be thrown away as unserviceable."* In that single sentence are concentrated all the tangled interpretative questions posed by Bonhoeffer's uncompleted work: Is "soon" tomorrow, or the end of history? Who will throw the principles away, we or God? For what purposes are they "unserviceable"? For the purposes of Kant, who wanted them to be *first and last* words of moral thought? Or are they unserviceable even as *first* words, from which the exploration of concrete reality may begin? These questions, which we cannot help putting to Bonhoeffer, will never be answered since he never made up his mind about them. In reacting against Kantian universal prescriptivism he was undecided whether Ethics was tied to Kant's paradigm, and therefore unredeemable, or whether it could be refounded theologically. If in the apocalyptic moment of "Ethics as Formation" the very idea of a Christian Ethics looks like a subversive paradox, different impressions can be formed from later essays. We find that Ethics "prepares the way" for the ultimate by caring for the penultimate; that there is a moral reason "embedded in the natural," which itself is "determined by its orientation towards Christ"; that a "new kind of discernment . . . encompassed and pervaded by the commandment" brings "intellect, cognitive ability and attentive perception of context . . . into lively play."** But through all the uncertainties of a fertile mind denied the opportunity to draw its insights together, one central thesis is always maintained: human moral reason, however we understand it, can and must assume the "form" of the decisive moral fact of history, the life and death of Jesus Christ.

So much for "conforming"; what, then, is meant by "transforming"? Two indicators must suffice, both drawn from the

* Bonhoeffer, *Ethics*, 28–29.
**Bonhoeffer, *Ethics*, 94, 107, 237–38.

Christian rite of baptism, which is described theologically as "the seal of the Spirit." In the first place, baptism is *the full reconciliation of the individual agent with the acting community.* In the second place, it is *the full reconciliation of the immediately present self with the moral future.*

Existence in community is natural, not artificial, and so, therefore, is cooperative action. Individual personal identities are formed in the womb of interaction; we never begin and we never cease to identify ourselves by reference to those around us. But because our communities are historical entities, not timeless wombs, our self-identification is formed in relation to others' actions, in sympathy with them or in alienation from them. (Communities, too, are agents, and relate to one another in the same way, implicitly cooperating with other communities and resisting them, as their practical projects coincide or collide.) That is the ground of the uneasy relation that all societies have with their members. Alienation, playing out the logic of the conflict between Socrates and the laws of Athens, is not an expression of pure individuality but a state of unhappy socialization. The difficulty of thinking about the individual in society is not created by any doubt that individual and the society "arise together," defining one another from the beginning, but by a doubt as to whether they have a common historical *destiny,* so that they can finally be reconciled. The tendency of the individual self-consciousness to pull apart and define its goals over against community, the thrust to individualize selfhood, though conceived within the womb of community, seems doomed to threaten participation in community. The individual is a rebellious child, threatening to slay its parent. How, then, may the individual be fulfilled in community, and the community fulfilled in its individual members? Most modern political thought has wished to answer that question (the sociologically based thought of the early nineteenth century alone excepted), and has tended to proceed one-sidedly from individual aspirations and to imagine the community as a kind of agreement among mature individuals to realize ends in common, reviving in modern forms the classical idea of the community of law as a rational contractual agreement to secure common interests. From the artificiality of this proposal, resolutely pursued over four centuries from Buchanan to Rawls, most of the political weakness of our civilization derives.

In baptism we see an individual act that grounds an identity, precisely as the contractarian tradition hypothesized, by voluntary and free assumption of a fuller personal identity within a community. But the common identity is not *itself* formed by such an act, nor by a series of such acts, undertaken reciprocally or by agreement. It preexists its members, formed by the identity of Christ himself, and each individual member who freely assumes that identity is inducted into it by the divine Spirit that dwelt in Christ. In speaking of this identity we refer initially and provisionally to "the church," but potentially we refer to humanity itself, since the church understands itself as the first-fruits of the human race, looking forward to a fuller and total realization of what is presently realized proleptically. Bonhoeffer described this relation of individual to community as *Stellvertretung*, "representation," meaning that each member "stands for" the other, just as the Christ "stands for" the whole human race and its destiny. Such an expression is, of course, liable to misunderstanding. Taking on the identity of another in preference to my own—what can that mean? It seems to portend a heroic act of self-conquest, or perhaps self-destruction in the cause of the other, unless we can conceive how a personal identity we have been given can *bear within it* an opening to share the identity of another. In other words, we have to break imaginatively with the hard, encrusted individual identity that starts out by making bargains with others equally hard and encrusted, and we must discover that from the beginning our identities were expansive, questioning, in search of answers and growth that only the social presence of other identities could give. Mutual "representation," then, cannot be the foundation of community; but community can be the foundation of mutual representation. The church that takes form as mutual representation is given, not constructed.

It has come to reality at the christological moment of history, together with the unique human agent who made that conception of community possible. The church is described in the New Testament as the "body of Christ."

From which there follows a second point about baptism: imprinting a new beginning to life on one who is already living a life both physical and spiritual, it has to do with *realizing moral agency*. It is repentance and faith, a conscious reflection on the defectiveness of the agency in which the individual has existed unreflectively, "an appeal to God for a good conscience," as the New Testament puts it (1 Pet. 3:21 ESV), which is to say, for fulfillment of agency in the Spirit. Baptism is the ritual action of "conversion," referring not to a biographically contingent crisis, something that may occur in the course of one person's experience and not in that of another, but to an essential moment in agency as such. The idea of moral conversion as a radical religious experience was current in the pagan mystery religions of the ancient world, and the philosophical reflections they inspired came to be part of Judaic monotheism. All ideas of conversion, philosophical and religious, associate it with recognition of the reality of death. The moral anticipation of death, like conversion itself, is a theme of ancient philosophy, which counseled it in order to overcome the terror of extinction. Death, the ultimate demoralizing force, brought the exertion of moral agency to nothing. What such Jewish figures as John the Baptist added to this existing cluster of concerns was to associate them with the idea of a fulfillment of history. Doubt over the form of history had subverted moral confidence in the law, but a new revelation of the form of history was at hand, empowering new moral beginnings through the dawning christological event. The life and action of the individual is imprinted with the christological moment of history; it appropriates the promise for agency that lies within the proclamation of God's kingdom.

So in baptism, in the third place, future history lays claim on individuals, who acknowledge the claim by living toward history's fulfillment. The immediate prospects may be obscure, and the time given to any one person on earth may be short. Yet the future makes a claim that does not hang on actuarial calculations. Whether for years or for minutes, the duty of continuing, sustaining moral sight, resisting the tendencies of natural being to forget what has been given, is made possible by anticipation. The New Testament moral category of *endurance* focuses on that particular task: once granted a clear view of the moral direction of the future, we may maintain that view against distractions, internal and external. "The world" (i.e., the routine and commonplace), "the flesh" (the tendency to lose the capacity for effort), and "the devil" (the presence of objective threat, rendering purposes meaningless) all expose us to a loss of clear direction. But life in its natural extension from youth to age can be understood as a coherent purpose that ensures a coherent subject; it is possible to conclude life on the same convictions about God's work in history with which we began, and therefore to conclude it *as the same person* that we began.

The Personal Fulfillment of Human Life

Perhaps there is nothing of which moral skepticism has left us so hauntingly doubtful as whether an individual can be one and the same person from one end of life to the other. Yet that can never be more than a *doubt*. And as a doubt it may be treated as dismissible, for it is simply not possible to think the thesis of personal discontinuity to a consistent conclusion; offering us no purchase on ourselves, the idea of personal discontinuity offers us no purchase on anything else, and therefore—while abstractly it might be "true"—cannot be *understood*. If I ask whether I am still the same person that I was, my question is badly formed. The right way to ask it is: How can I come to *envisage* my life as a moral whole? To see oneself in that light is something very close to the classical ideal of *eudaimonia*, "happiness," which Solon thought could only be attributed to a life when it was finished, and which Augustine, in a very different sense, agreed could only be enjoyed in a state of eternal rest.

It is difficult, when one is old, to recall the life one has lived in all its details; it is impossible, when one is young, to imagine with any concreteness the life one has yet to live. Even when life has been concluded, it is difficult for a third party to see it as a whole. Consider the problems faced by the literary art of biography, the focus of great moral hopes in the twentieth century and once predicted to replace the novel as the dominant medium of moral instruction. But fiction had picked only the low-hanging fruit of moral reflection; it had focused on crises that could force a character to declare itself, on trials and influences that could draw it out from its social background to take shape as a definite person, and then . . . "they lived happily ever after." Biography wrestled with the much more difficult task of imagining the excellence of a human life as it appeared from birth to death. The early chapters, trawling through domestic and educational trivia, the closing pages detailing the ravages of age and declining health—these challenge a biographer's capacity to unify the life around its moments of greatest significance. For in early youth and declining age nature intrudes on historical existence, and the greatest biographers are those who are capable of letting nature appear in a historical light. Taking the measure of this challenge, we can appreciate the origins of biography as a form of religious writing, finding the unity of a life in the pilgrimage of the soul from the City of Destruction to the Heavenly City, treating discipline and suffering as positive accomplishments and reaching the decisive moment only at the very end, when "the trumpets sounded for him on the other side."

Karl Barth showed great perspicacity in identifying the un-formed but unavoidable question of the overall shape of our lives as a perennial sign of the providential work of God sustaining nature in history.* In thinking of a whole life, we encounter

* Barth, *Church Dogmatics* III/3, §49.3, 226–38.

the same delicate dialectic as in thinking of the world as both "nature" and "history." A life is one act; its consistency must be evident if it is to be unified. Yet it is constantly involved in irreversible changes, some natural, some moral. It must have a beginning that is different from its end and a direction leading from one to the other without going round in circles. A personal life is not "one" in the sense that a natural organism is one, a series of repetitive functions. To the observer it may become "one," as a historical fact is one: once transacted, it is a fixed and unchangeable unit in the record of the objective past. That observer's point of view is adopted by the portraitist. Think of Holbein's *Henry VIII*—a complex depiction, with many references to imagined or actual realities of sixteenth-century absolutism, all brought together in one personal figure, caught in a posture that declares the unarguable facticity of political power. But the unity of a historical fact is not the unity of a living person. For a person the sameness of life consists in constant submission to circumstantial change. When Jesus was asked, "Teacher, what good thing must I do that I may have eternal life?" (Matt. 19:16 RV), the answer expected and given was about how to live in a clear direction while always on the move. Eternal life that is *sought*, is sought to be lived eternally, and therefore always sought *as a goal*, however much its possession may be effectively realized. But it is not an alien goal, a horizon of becoming something else. It follows from the doing and being of life, a conclusion that unifies the self's lived experiences.

This dialectic is beautifully explored in one of Kierkegaard's shorter and less celebrated literary works.* The engaging essay *Repetition*, marked by all the eclectic formal features typical of his early writing techniques of framing, multiple authorial voices, autobiographical content reflected on fictional characters, humorous narrative, theatrical criticism, introspective reli-

---

* Søren Kierkegaard, "Repetition," in *Kierkegaard's Writings VI*, ed. and trans. Howard V. Hong and Edna H. Hong (Princeton: Princeton University Press, 1983), 125–231.

gious meditation, etc.—is guided by a single philosophical question: How can the life of an individual achieve self-sameness?
The thesis "Repetition is reality, and it is the seriousness of life"
is the starting point. But this poses the question how repetition
can possibly *occur* in the life of the spirit. Each experience we
"repeat" is different the next time we repeat it. Merely recol-
lecting and retaining the past achieves, at most, an "anaesthetis-
ing uniformity." The answer offered is that only acute suffering
allows self-repetition *in self-transcendence.* "Becoming oneself
again" is a repetition peculiarly reserved for the sufferer. Job,
the paradigm sufferer, refuses to yield to the view of himself that
he is offered by his comforters but clings resolutely to a self-
experience in which his "passion of freedom . . . (is) not stifled
or tranquilized by a false expression." He cannot repent what he
has been, except before God, for God can give him back what
he has been in true self-knowledge. His "trial of probation" calls
forth "the firmness which he is able to eschew all crafty ethical
evasions." Looking solely to God to reconcile past and future,
he reaffirms himself, ending where he began, but in a different
way. He has received everything back—"double." Job's suffer-
ings, Kierkegaard encourages us to think, are by no means over
at the end of the book, and yet, because they have been grasped
as a probation, they can be received differently, as a reward.

Here, we may be tempted to think, is a modern version of
the old Aristotelian-Thomist account of "character" as formed
by repetition of acts that express given virtues. But the modern version is importantly different from the old. Where the
Thomist account had a pedagogical focus, viewing repetition as
a training that formed habits that would become second nature
and allow one to act instinctively, on Kierkegaard's account repetition is never left behind. If repetition, on the older account,
was a precursor to virtue, Kierkegaard is famous for treating
virtue and its "ethical" ambitions as a precursor to faith, which
is the true life of the spirit, the inner side of "freedom." Job's
established virtues, which surely scored high on the Aristotelian scale of magnanimity, were of no service in his changed

circumstances; they belonged to the role he had lost, not to his innermost life as a sufferer. New roles need new virtues, but faith repeats itself, and in repetition acquires the form of "faithfulness" in the midst of total change. That is how the person, the liver of life in strength and weakness, in usefulness and helplessness, may be grasped concretely, the whole of life a probation of one and the same character, a probation inseparable from life in the Spirit.

The Mutual Service of Ethics and Theology

It is time to look back over the journey we have taken. We have explored the dependence of moral reason on the being and time of the world, and our own role as personal agents within the agency of the divine Spirit. A "moral order," if we are to speak of such a thing to any effect, must be spoken of in this way, too, as an ordering within history, not only as an ordering within nature. The agency of the divine Spirit in world and time is the context in which we conceive our own agency as effective. This service, then, theology can claim to render Ethics: it describes conditions for the security of moral reasoning in the world and history.

In setting out we suggested *en passant* that Ethics is "somewhere near the center" of the range of topics embraced by "natural theology." If natural theology is not to be conceived in a revisionist manner as a reconstruction of theology on rationalist terms, it must be an *apologetic* undertaking, offering the support and assistance of natural reason to revealed theology, demonstrating the place of revelation within a general framework of intelligibility. I close with a remark or two about this. Kant, whom we now mention for the last time, conceived that such an apologetic service to theology could be rendered *only* by Ethics. The classic arguments for the existence of God based on motion, causation, necessity, possibility, and form proved nothing at all, he argued; but moral reason *presupposes* the truths of God, the soul, and eternal life, and while this can never be a proof such as those arguments were sometimes thought to supply, it is a confirmation of faith if the promise of a goal of history is something Ethics, as such, is inevitably on the lookout for.

That one does not *deduce* the existence of God from any truth about other things in the world or relations that obtain there has since become accepted common ground. But reasoning about the world has come to seem rather less dependent on deduction than once appeared, and rather more upon induction, pressing behind appearances to the conditions of appearance. In such probing explorations of the world's reality, thought must ask about the status of the various forms of intelligibility on display there; arguments that start from the phenomena of motion, causation, necessity, possibility, form, and so on may be interpreted more sympathetically as pursuing just such interrogations. Philosophy may declare such interrogations inconclusive, not because they are ill conceived but simply because not everything that can be asked can be answered. The universe of knowledge is not a closed system where all loose ends are tied up. The "moral argument" for God, the soul, and eternal life thus conforms precisely to the shape of the other classic arguments: forms of intelligibility that the world offers are questioned about the reality that lies behind them. The practical question is then, can we *live* with such unresolved questions? Kant's claim for the moral argument was that it showed we could not live that way. Practical reason itself is subverted if the appearance of ultimate practical ends cannot be relied on. For practical reason implies moral consistency, and moral consistency requires the promise of a future to vindicate its relation to the world of action. Kant did not know how a rational being could adopt morality while in doubt of an ultimate end of striving. We have to choose either to live by moral faith or to embrace moral cynicism.

The conclusion of the moral argument is, of course, that same "God of the philosophers" who is famously (and perhaps too destructively) derided by Pascal. The moral argument does not somehow get us past the logic of history and revelation, which is that if God is to be known, God must disclose himself. What the God of the philosophers amounts to is a kind of conceptual map-reference, by which the revelation of the God of Abraham, Isaac, and Jacob, when such is given us, may be plotted onto experience. It is the location of a reasonable expectation and hope. So the promise of a goal of history that positive theology lays claim to is a promise Ethics knows how to welcome and locate. There is no exceeding the limits of apologetics; Ethics can rid religious belief of apparent moral irrelevance, but it cannot clothe it in necessity. Yet to those who know themselves called to believe as they live, and to live as they believe, the conceptual support that it can offer is not negligible.

But at this point the service rendered by Ethics to theology can be returned. For Ethics itself, and the practical reasoning it deals with, have a habit of disappearing from view. In a scientific or purely descriptive organization of knowledge moral reason will be lost sight of and Ethics left without a home, for it is concerned with the active dimension of life that lies beyond these special projects of description and is never captured by the lens of any of them. Whatever reality we observe, and whatever our means of observing it, the question of how life may be conducted reasonably in relation to it lies beyond the scope of that observation. Life itself, of course, does not disappear from the human world when it disappears from the world of organized knowledge. But if the claims of knowledge and the demands of life pull apart too sharply, our capacity both for life and knowledge is weakened. Knowledge is left without a knower, suspended on an impersonal point of view that no concrete person ever occupies, while life is lived without informed self-reflection, and hence without power of intelligent self-direction. Ethics, as a branch of philosophical knowledge, cannot do without its basis in existential wonder.

Theology, in teaching us to bless God for our creation, preservation, and all the blessings of this life, which is to say, for nature, for history, and for our concrete interpersonal existence, anchors us in wonder, guards us from losing ourselves in disillusioned bewilderment. To take a recent painful example: when wondering how to live in the midst of a dangerous pandemic, we called on the specialist knowledge of epidemiologists and virologists; but this, indispensable as it inevitably was, was not sufficient to guide reasonable decisions. "Following the science" (as the slogan had it) was a limiting constraint, not a course of action that could simply be pursued. Science has no direction that it has not borrowed from life itself; it is simply the observation of natural regularities. In such a crisis we have to reflect on our priorities for common life, and we reasonably expect Ethics to come to our aid with some basic affirmations about what matters most. But what guidance can Ethics offer, if its key points of reference threaten to disappear? What we saw in the crisis now behind us was a familiar phenomenon: repeated assertions of value, strident, unreasoned, and incompatible. The priority of the protection of human life was assumed, as was the necessity for resort to biotechnology. Neither of these instinctive assumptions was in the least supported by the broader descriptions of biological life on earth that have been current in our age or by the "green" policies they have inspired. So we developed an unresolvable tension between the urgent need to "defeat" the virus and our other great cultural concern, the need to "save" the wider planetary ecosystem. We endured what seemed to us a large wastage of human life in the pandemic, but suppressed the knowledge that the ecosystem might have benefited enormously if it had been considerably larger. Which is not an argument for favoring the planet rather than human lives, or vice versa. It is merely an expression of wonder that no argument on either side was heard. On Mondays, Wednesdays, and Fridays we defeated the virus; on Tuesdays, Thursdays, and Saturdays we saved the planet; and we had no Sabbath wisdom to join these two all-engrossing and mutually conflicting commitments into a coherent moral posture. Has the human race reached the point where it can no longer argue with conviction for what its cultural instincts tell it strongly that it ought to do? What is the future for a race whose brain has so lost touch with its hands and legs? It is at *that* point that any service Ethics may have rendered theology can be more profoundly repaid as a service rendered by theology to Ethics. Theology—or, to speak more precisely, the prophetic word of good news—comes to the aid of human moral reason where it feels the ground falling away under its feet. It assures it of the validity of moral thought in a world where the meaning of history is not perspicuous. Which is to say, theology comes to the aid of human existence itself.

Index

action: and agency, 55–58; cooperation, 128–32, 141; creation, 82–83, 88, 93; deeds, 10, 68, 74, 76, 130; faith, 137; finitude, 129; freedom, 131; God, 98–99, 128–30; and the good, 10–13, 82, 83; and history, 88, 122–23; human, 128–29; moral experience, 93; original, 82–83; and the person, 56–59, 64–65; practical reason, 11–15; and time, 88; of will, 10

Adam, 7–8

admiration, 13, 18–19, 25

agency: and action, 55, 57, 58; and baptism, 143; cooperative, 128–32; disappearance, 55–56, 127–28; faith, 137; and freedom, 18; God, 30, 99, 128–30, 132; the good, 29–32, 127; and history, 123, 143–44; human, 18, 29, 31–32, 137–44; justification, 127; moral, 60, 143; the person, 29, 58–59,

62, 73–75; recognition, 56–57; Spirit, 132, 133, 138

"analytic" in Kant, 17, 63

Anschauung, 22

Anscombe, Elizabeth, 51

anticipation, 41–45, 125

Arendt, Hannah, 96

Aristotle, 7, 13, 18, 53, 112n

Augustine, 8–9, 10, 13n, 21, 23, 38, 41, 56, 69, 145

axiology, 21. *See also* values

Balthasar, Hans Urs von, 124–25

baptism, 76, 141–44

Barth, Karl, 65, 82, 83, 85, 96, 98, 132, 145

beauty, 8, 25

being: beyond, 13; creation, 86; and evil, 8–9; and the good, 8–9, 34, 35, 85–86, 88–93; nonbeing, 8–9; recurrence, 77; and time, 85–86; values, 22n

benefit, 82

bioethics, 79